D1584686

BRADFORD ON AVON: PAST AND PRESENT

*Cover: View of Bradford on Avon looking south-west from Whitehill;
Photograph by Adam Tegetmeier, September 1993.*

B.C.H.E. – LIBRARY

00087652

*Lumbering Saxon ox-wagons beat out the track to and from
the river – crossing to form what we call Silver Street.
The building-line is, at latest, medieval.*

BRADFORD on AVON PAST and PRESENT

Harold Fassnidge

Photography by Adam Tegetmeier

EX LIBRIS PRESS

First published in 1988
This new, revised, expanded and reset edition
Published in 1993 by
Ex Libris Press
1 The Shambles
Bradford on Avon
Wiltshire

Typeset in 11 point Palatino
Design and typesetting by Ex Libris Press

Cover printed by Shires Press, Trowbridge
Printed by Redwood Books, Trowbridge, Wiltshire

BATH COLLEGE OF
HIGHER EDUCATION
NEWTON PARK LIBRARY

CLASS NO.
942.31 FAS

SUPPLIER
DAW

DISCARD

© Harold Fassnidge and Adam Tegetmeier

ISBN 0 948578 62 9

Publisher's Note: A royalty based upon sales of this book will be donated to Bradford on Avon Museum Society.

CONTENTS

ACKNOWLEDGMENTS

My grateful thanks go to the staff of the Wiltshire Record Office, of the Local Studies Section of the Wiltshire Library and Museum Service and of the library of the Wiltshire Archaeological and Natural History Society, who could not have been more helpful, and also to the following who have helped in various ways: The Rev. Francis Bell, Mrs Mollie Dotesio, Mrs Celia Feane, Mrs Margaret Dobson, John Fassnidge of the National Army Museum, Robin and Barbara Harvey, Alan Hicks, Colin Johns of Wilts County Council, Jim King, Roger Mawby, John Sargant, former Vicar of Christ Church, Mrs Pamela Slocombe, Mrs Gillian Spriggs of Bradford on Avon Preservation Trust, Jack Stafford, Malcolm Thomas, Librarian of the Religious Society of Friends, and Miss Joyce Uncles.

I have also drawn upon the following unpublished material kindly made available to me:

Christopher Moody's *History of Leigh Park Hotel*
Ivor Slocombe's *The Christ Church Schools*
Matthew Slocombe's university dissertation (1987), *Clothiers to Gentlemen: the development of the Yerbury family and the Belcombe estate at Bradford on Avon, Wilts.*
John C Shehan's *History of the Bradford on Avon Town Club* and his paper on Hall's Charity.

ABOUT THE AUTHOR

Harold Fassnidge is a barrister who spent most of his working life in the Diplomatic Service. He fell in love with Bradford on Avon many years ago when on home leave from India and on retirement went there to live. He co-edited *Bradford on Avon: A Pictorial Record* (published in 1983 by Wiltshire Library and Museum Service) and in 1986 his monograph *The Quakers of Melksham* (published in 1992) was awarded first prize in the Lloyd's Bank/County Council 1985/6 Wiltshire History Competition.

PREFACE

As one of the team of honorary guides for Bradford on Avon Preservation Trust I have over a number of years had the pleasure of conducting parties of visitors around the town, not all of them from Britain, not all having much knowledge of our national history or of where local history fits into the pattern. In putting together this account I have borne in mind the questions I have been asked at various times by non-historian visitors and have assumed that the reader will have no great knowledge of English history, political or social. My intention therefore has been to present an accurate up-to-date picture of this attractive small town and its past mainly for the general reader. But I hope that the dedicated local historian also will find something of value.

Harold Fassnidge
Bradford on Avon
May 1988

PREFACE TO THE SECOND EDITION

Developments since the first edition was published are recorded in the new text; with the closure of the Avon Industrial Polymers factory and the Darlington company's mushroom-growing operation more radical changes are imminent.

An account which does not say something about the way ordinary people lived says too little. The additional chapters I have added in this edition are based on scraps of information I have accumulated in my serendipitous rummagings in the archives. They are not exhaustive; I hope they will encourage others to delve deeper.

Harold Fassnidge
Bradford on Avon
April 1993

INTRODUCTION

Bradford on Avon begins where the Cotswolds end. It lies at the most southerly tip, a semi-circular escarpment reaching steeply southwards to the valley below. From riverside up to ancient Budbury a charming medley of stone houses and cottages of almost every style covers the slopes. On Newtown, Middle Rank and Tory tiers of houses form a kind of grandstand, from which to see, and be seen by, those in the valley below in mutual agreeable contemplation. Down by where the town bridge now stands (and where, a millennium and more ago, Saxon Bradford began) Saxon ox-wagons once crossed and re-crossed the broad ford which gave the town its name, and lumbering up the hillsides beyond created the winding ways we call now Silver Street and St Margaret's Street.

In 1913 the poet Edward Thomas, cycling through, paused to enjoy the scene:

> I dismounted by the empty Lamb Inn, with a statue of a black-faced lamb over its porch, and sat on the bridge. The Avon ran swift but calm and dull, down under the bridge and away westward. The town hill rises from off the water, covered as with scales with stone houses of countless varieties of blackened grey and many gables, and so steep that the roofs of one horizontal street are only just higher than the doorsteps of the one above. A brewery towers from the mass at the far side and, near the top, a factory with the words FOR SALE printed on the roof in huge letters. And the smoke of factories blew across the town. The hilltop above the houses is crested with beeches and rooks' nests against the blue. The narrow space between the foot of the hill and the river is occupied by private gardens, a church and its churchyard yews and chestnuts and by a tall empty factory based on the river bank itself, with a notice TO LET.

From *In Pursuit of Spring*, re-published in 1981 by Wildwood House Ltd.

Three quarters of a century later the scene is not greatly changed. The Lamb Inn has gone, and in its place stands a factory building. The houses are, for the most part, not nearly so blackened. The towering brewery in

Newtown has closed long since, the building it occupied, now converted to flats, still prominent but rivalled by the Rope Walk development. The tall factory (Abbey Mill), relic of the dead clothing industry, is still there, but has not been unoccupied since 1915 when it was taken over for rubber manufacture. No longer does the smoke of factories blow across the town.

In its day Bradford on Avon was an important manufacturing town, a leader in the clothing industry. From the earliest times good quality wool had always been abundant, producing income and clothing for rich and poor alike. From the fourteenth century (when the English, helped by a medieval brain-drain from Flanders, first learnt to spin and weave their own wool for sale as good quality finished cloth instead of sending it abroad for processing) up to the eighteenth century, Bradfordians, for the most part, prospered and some of them got very rich.

Like every other town and village Bradford on Avon streets were once filthy with garbage and ordure from man and beast. On at least two occasions that we know of, in 1609 and 1646, the town was afflicted with the plague, so sorely (for twenty long weeks on the earlier occasion) that towns and villages as far away as Chippenham had to be specially taxed to help out. Today's visitor, happily, does not need the reassurance offered in local directories in the eighteenth and nineteenth centuries that the town's situation was such that all impurities after passing down its sloping streets, were immediately carried off by the waters of the Avon...

Bradford on Avon was largely spared the spate of destruction which took place elsewhere in the name of progress in the 1960s, and since then the greater part of the town has been designated a conservation area. So, for the foreseeable future, Bradford's nooks and crannies, alleys and back-streets and above all its lovely old buildings, with their occasional little surprises, will continue to charm us all. Long may it be so!

1.
CELTS, ROMANS, SAXONS and NORMANS

Celts

The West Country was colonised by Celts from mainland Europe some two and a half millennia ago and traces of Celtic settlements are to be found all over Wiltshire and neighbouring counties. In Bradford on Avon in the Iron Age (in Britain roughly five hundred years before the birth of Christ) the high ground on the north side of the town was inhabited. In 1969 what had previously been thought to be a prehistoric religious site, barrow or burial ground was found to be the remains of an Iron Age fort. Excavation showed the defences to consist of a bank with double ditches in front. Iron Age pottery and other objects were found. In 1986, when the site at what used to be called Bed and Bolster field at Budbury Farm was about to become a housing development, county archaeologists did a hurried dig and found more pieces of Iron Age pottery. Evidence of extensive earthworks suggested protection of a community occupying about ten acres.

Romans

There was a Roman or Romano-British settlement on the same spot and to the north-west of it but it must have been small. The area was heavily wooded and well off the paved road which ran through *Cunetio* (Mildenhall) and *Verlucio* (Sandy Lane) to *Aquae Sulis* (Bath). The Roman settlers probably came by way of Bath, which was an important Roman town from the first century on. It would be natural for them to settle and farm where their Iron Age predecessors did and doubtless the commanding views of the territory to the south impressed them. Until it was built on in 1986, Budbury Ridge retained the vestiges of what appeared to be a typical Roman *vallum* (rampart). Many Roman coins and fragments of other artefacts have been found in the area.

In Bath, as elsewhere, the senior ranks both military and civilian will have been Rome-based and patrician, the lower ones locally recruited. Who or what the first Roman or Romano-British residents of Bradford on Avon were we can only surmise from such archaeological evidence as has become available. This evidence reveals a high degree of sophistication, particularly in the third century AD. But whether they were thoroughly Romanised Britons or of Roman descent through intermarriage or a mixed community of both is uncertain.

In 1976 the remains of a Romano-British house of some quality were discovered at Budbury. A dig[1] led by Alison Borthwick of the Archaeological Section of Wiltshire County Council yielded evidence of construction between the second and fourth centuries. A coin of AD 70 (Vespasian) was found at the lowest level excavated and post-holes near by suggested occupation about that date. In its heyday, perhaps the third century AD to judge by fragments of glass, painted plaster and household equipment found at the higher levels and the existence of a bath-house, it was the home of a prosperous landowner. Later it fell on evil times, seemingly given over to use for grain-drying and storage and at one point suffering fire damage. Of the many Roman coins found in the Budbury area, the latest is of the time of the emperor Valens (AD 364-378). But if the Romans gave the settlement a name it has not come down to us. What we do have from those days is the name of the river: the word Avon derives from the Old British *abona* from which modern Welsh derives *afon*.

A Truly Saxon Town

It was the Saxons who founded and named the town; and of the many English Bradfords Bradford on Avon, with seniority from AD 652, takes pride of place in the records. (The Yorkshire Bradford first appears in 1086, some four centuries later, when William the Conqueror's diligent surveyors and enumerators recorded it in the Domesday Book). More than thirteen centuries ago a battle was fought here. The *Anglo-Saxon Chronicle* records that in AD 652 Cenwalh, king of Wessex, fought at *Bradenforda be afne* (literally the broad ford on the river). It may well be that the battle was where the town bridge now stands. From time immemorial this has been the site of a ford and, indeed, it continued to be used as such until the present embankments were created. *Kelly's Directories* up to 1900 stated that the river could be crossed dryshod here.

Here, most probably, was the broad ford on the Avon which, thirteen centuries ago, gave the town its name. The river was fordable at this point up to the beginning of the present century.

What gave rise to the dispute or against whom Cenwalh was fighting is uncertain because the chroniclers do not agree. But less than a century before (until the Saxon victory at Dyrham in AD 577) the town had been within British (Welsh) territory, a short distance beyond the north-west frontier of Wessex. To the north and west dispossessed Welshmen will have nursed resentment. What the Saxons had taken from them had been quite literally the land of their fathers and reprisals will doubtless have been attempted from time to time; so it seems likely that it was against them for control of the river, a natural frontier and highway.

The earliest Saxon settlement will have been on the south side of the river and its broad ford, probably occupying the high ground of what is now St Margaret's Hill, St Margaret's Place and St Margaret's Villas. Once the river was securely under their control the Saxons could cross over to the other bank and settle there. According to tradition the monastery or abbey known to have been established in Saxon times was located on the north bank roughly where the church of the Holy Trinity was later built. The names of Abbey House and Abbey Mills, built near what was once called Abbey Yard, remind us of this tradition.

Precisely when the West Saxons built their little church (of which more later) and how much the present building owes to the original one is uncertain, and the question has been the subject of much learned discussion. Best opinion seems to be that it was rebuilt in the reign of Aethelred II (978-1016) (Aethelred the Unredy), perhaps because the original structure had, Saxon-fashion, been made of wood and was by then crumbling away. But we do know from what William of Malmesbury wrote in 1125 that *it was said* to have been built by Bishop Aldhelm. Aldhelm, (c 640-709), a Benedictine monk of royal descent who subsequently became the first bishop of Sherborne, was almost certainly the founder of the monastery, of which he was abbot, and it may be that a church was erected near by to encourage the laity. (Christianity was still a novelty to Saxons with King Cenwalh himself only a recent convert).

The little church retains to this day one direct link with its founder. When Aldhelm died on a visit to Doulting, some twenty miles to the southwest, his body was carried back to his old home, the abbey at Malmesbury. By order of Ecquin, Bishop of Worcester, stone crosses were set up at the seven resting places on the way, of which Bradford on Avon was one; and what remains of the Bradford cross – two pieces – may be seen over the altar.

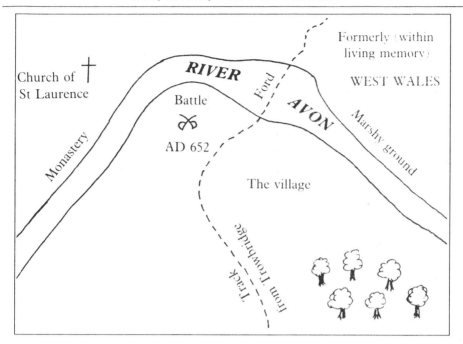

Bradford on Avon in Bishop Aldhelm's lifetime (AD 640-709).

In 1988, the year of the millennium of the death of St Dunstan (*c* 909-988), it was appropriate to recall that both he and his enemy King Aethelred are part of Bradford's history. It was at an assembly here in the year 954 that under Eadred, King of Wessex, whose chief adviser he was, Dunstan was made Bishop of Worcester. In due course (in 959) he became Archbishop of Canterbury[2] under his friend and ally King Edgar (959-975). Dunstan was as much politician as priest and when Edgar died in 975 he it was who settled the question of succession by arbitrarily crowning Edgar's son Edward ('the Martyr') in preference to Aethelred the Unredy, his half-brother, thus incurring Aethelred's undying enmity. Three years later Edward was murdered at Corfe Castle at the instigation of Aethelred's mother Elfrida so that Aethelred could take his place on the throne.

With Aethelred king, Dunstan's political power was over. But perhaps his moral influence survived, even after his death. The Manor of Bradford, comprising the monastery, the town and the neighbouring villages, was royal property. Troubled in conscience about how he had come to the throne, in the year 1001 Aethelred gave it to the Abbey of

Shaftesbury 'as a safe refuge for the nuns against the insults of the Danes, and a hiding place also for the relics of the blessed martyr St. Edward and the rest of the saints.' In the event the monastery was sacked and totally destroyed soon afterwards, most probably by Aethelred's old adversary Canute, who, as we know from the *Anglo-Saxon Chronicles*, raided up the river Frome in 1015. If Aethelred was sincere it seems odd that the abbey at Bradford on, or very near the bank of a river, should be thought safer than the one at Shaftesbury; perched as it was on very high ground the latter was surely much less vulnerable. Was this yet another misjudgement of the kind that earned Aethelred his Saxon nickname *Unredy* – the Ill-advised? Or did he secretly hope that by putting Edward's bones out of sight in remote Bradford he would thereby put them out of mind?

The Norman Heritage

The Norman Conquest created no great upheaval in Bradford. The Abbey of Shaftesbury continued to hold the manor of Bradford (42 hides – about 5,000 acres) and it would appear from the Domesday Book that at least some Anglo-Saxon landowners transferred their allegiance to William.

By the middle of the twelfth century the Normans built a larger church (now Holy Trinity) alongside the little Saxon one. Some of its Norman features remain.

To the Normans we also owe the town bridge, which, much repaired and restored over the centuries, nevertheless retains two late Norman (thirteenth century) arches; they are the ones nearest the south bank. The bridge as it is today is really two bridges in the sense that its width was doubled by the building alongside of another one in the latter half of the eighteenth century. If there was a bridge before the Normans came it was probably a wooden one – a 'tree-bridge' like the one which gave neighbouring Trowbridge its name. But the Saxons may well have been content to splash bridgeless across the ford. Before the embankments were constructed around the turn of the present century horse-drawn vehicles could, and often did, use the ford for preference. An engraving of 1830 from a drawing by W Westall shows the unembanked slopes which made this possible.

Right up to the time of the widening of the bridge reluctance to spend money on it was a recurring problem and this reluctance is documented back to 1400 (when the Pope himself intervened); so the ford was doubtless seen from time to time as safer. Like fourteenth century Barton bridge, leading to and from Barton Farm and the tithe barn, it seems to have been built without parapets; and that from time to time a citizen took a tumble over the edge into the river we gather from a minute of 1502 calling for a 'copying' the lack of which was 'to the grave danger of the King's people'.

Bradford on Avon lies on a major traffic route (the long-promised bypass is not now expected to be built before the end of the century) and the old bridge has stood up to it well. Since 1992 the heaviest vehicles have been banned from using it.

The population of the manor of Bradford at the time of the Norman Conquest was, according to Canon Jones, about 700, of whom some three to four hundred lived in the town itself. He based his calculation on the Domesday record; the population included (in descending order of social status) 33 *burgesses* (town dwellers), 40 *bordarii* (husbandmen or cottagers with holdings of, say, 15 to 20 acres), 22 hog-keepers, 18 *coliberti* (freedmen who continued to owe service) 36 *villani* (villagers, unfree, being owned by their feudal lord, unable to own land but allowed to farm it for themselves) and nine *serfs* (bondmen owned by their feudal lord). There were two mills and a market. There was also a vineyard of about an acre (one *arpen*).

The only king known to have visited Bradford was a Norman one, the egregious King John (1199-1216) who found himself here in August 1216 in the course of his armed struggle with the barons who a year before had forced Magna Charta on him. Unsuccessful and very sick he died two months later.

NOTES

1. Notes on the dig are held in the Archaeological Section, Wilts County Council.
2. It was as archbishop that Dunstan was presiding over the *Witenagemot* (Assembly of the Wise Men) at Calne in the year 978 when according to the *Anglo-Saxon Chronicles*:

> All the chief Witan of the English nation fell from an upper chamber except the holy Archbishop Dunstan who alone supported himself on a beam. Some were grievously wounded and some did not excape with life.

Dunstan's friends proclaimed a miracle. His enemies (of whom he had many) claimed that he had arranged for the supporting timbers to be sawn almost through as a means of silencing the opposition.

2.
THE MIDDLE AGES
AND BEYOND

Peace and Prosperity

From the beginning Bradford had had what was needed to sustain life in comparative comfort; the means of good and durable shelter from the stone (jurassic oolite) never more than a few feet from the surface and food and clothing from the sheep grazing the surrounding chalk hills by day and folded by night to enrich the arable land. The long-drawn-out power struggle between barons and monarch which had begun in the reign of William the Conqueror's grandson Stephen was taking place elsewhere. Bradford was left undisturbed to grow and prosper, so much so that by the fourteenth century it was necessary to build a great barn as a storage place for the produce of Barton Farm and the tithe (one tenth) of the produce of all other land held in the manor of Bradford, payable in kind, to which the church was by law entitled.

In centuries to come some very large fortunes were made in the clothing industry and, as we shall see later, members of leading Bradford clothier families came to play their part on the national stage. But in the Middle Ages landowners were the rich and powerful ones.

Backwater though it still was in the late thirteenth century the town sometimes felt an eddy from the main stream. In 1295 King Edward I, at war with Scotland and Wales and under threat from continental Europe, found himself in dire financial straits. His remedy was to summon a parliament. He called representatives from every possible source of funds: earls, barons, archbishops and bishops, abbots and other church leaders, two knights from each shire and two representatives from each city and borough. It was the most representative assembly of its kind ever to be held in England up to then and for this reason is sometimes called the Model Parliament. Now designated as a borough (and a prosperous one at that) Bradford was obliged to comply and sent Thomas Dendans (or Dering) and William Wager; and the parliament having voted taxation, Bradford doubtless had to pay its whack. Thereafter the town was grateful to be left alone and, unlike neighbouring boroughs Calne, Chippenham, Devizes and Westbury, not called upon to be represented in parliament for the next 537 years.

Besides the tithe barn, and the charming stone bridge near by, one or two other buildings in the town still extant have their origins in the Middle Ages. Almost certainly one such is the little chapel or hermitage of St Mary the Virgin on Tory, though the earliest documentary date we have is 1540. In that year John Leland wrote in the course of his visit to the town: 'Ther is a chappelle on the highest place of the town as I entered.' A document of 1587 called it 'St Leonard's hermitage or chapel'. The cult of St Leonard, patron saint of prisoners, came to England with the Normans and the dedication may support a date as early even as the eleventh century. When Thomas Bush Saunders rebuilt it in 1870 only part of the east wall was still standing.

The fourteenth century tithe barn and (foreground left)
the fifteenth century granary.

Tithe-barn interior showing splendid cruck (curved beam) trusses.

The Chapel of St Mary the Virgin 'on the highest part of the town'.

At Priory House in Market Street the boundary wall bordering the road is medieval, all that remains of the substantial house built in the late 1400s by Thomas Rogers, Serjeant-at-Law. The present Priory House (see later) is the late Georgian extension originally built as a kitchen wing to the main house.

Number 11 Silver Street also has medieval origins. The east side of this L-shaped building incorporates the roof and other remains of a building of the period 1350-1450 set gable-end to the road. The buildings in The Shambles on the post office side (but not the post office itself) are of the same era. The timber facades are a later, probably seventeenth century, modernisation.

The house called Barton Farm goes back in part at least to the medieval period and possibly to Saxon times. From the fact that in the early sixteenth century it was called the manor house it seems likely that it, or its predecessor on the site, was the manor house of the manor of Bradford given, as we have seen, by Aethelred to the Abbess of Shaftesbury in the year 1001. The building called the granary is fifteenth century, the tithe barn fourteenth century. Barton Farm covered a large acreage on both sides of the river Avon linked from at least the fourteenth century by Barton Bridge. Barton Bridge may also once have served a track which led from Salisbury Plain through Bath to Bristol and the sea.

Reminders of early Bradford linger. The house in Church Street called The Chantry, which itself goes back in part to the early sixteenth century, recalls the pre-Reformation practice of endowing a church or chapel with lands or other source of income for the maintenance of a priest or priests to sing or say mass daily for the soul of the donor or for the souls of persons named by him or her. The present building is almost certainly on the site of the priest's house of the chantry founded by Thomas Horton in 1524, one of three such known to have existed here. St Margaret's Street and St Margaret's Hill derive their names from St Margaret's Hospital, a medieval institution whose precise location is unknown. During his visit John Leland noted: 'There is a litle streate over Bradford Bridge and at the ende of that is an hospitale of the Kinges of Englandes fundation.'

This may have been the leper hospital dedicated to St Margaret, known to have been founded in 1235 and to have been under the patronage of Shaftesbury Abbey. That it had existed for some years before Leland we know from a deed of about 1459 and also from a will of 1490 which bequeathed six shillings and eightpence to poor inmates. A number of old buildings, among them the old poorhouse, in what was then called St Margaret's Street (but is now called Frome Road) were demolished when the railway cutting was made. If what Leland saw was indeed the leper hospital, then a location away from the town centre, at that time on the north bank of the river, would be likely; so a reasonable guess would be that the old poorhouse had once been St Margaret's leper hospital. Further along Frome Road are St Catherine's Almshouses, a foundation of great antiquity. In pre-Reformation days (notably 1535) twelve poor persons were receiving six shillings and eightpence yearly in return for offering prayers for the soul of the founder of Shaftesbury Abbey and this gives credence to oral tradition that in the Middle Ages it was a large establishment with its own chapel and chaplain.

Woolley Street derives its name from the chapel of St Olave, known to have existed in the late thirteenth century. Over the years the name evolved from *Seynt Olesstret* (early fifteenth century) to *Tooley Street* (eighteenth century) to its present style.

Barton Bridge linked Barton farmhouse and barn with farmlands north of the river from at least the fourteenth century. Bradford on Avon Rowing Club boats are kept near by.

The Reformation

A king's marital and dynastic problems combined with the religious unrest which was disturbing all Christendom made for dangerous times. In Bradford the theological element of the equation gave rise to a burning at the stake; the political element brought to an end Shaftesbury Abbey's five centuries old manorial lordship.

Henry VIII, who up to 1535, notwithstanding his problems with the Vatican, saw himself as a good Catholic, was willing enough to allow a burning at the stake for the benefit of the soul of the heretic concerned. Thus it was that Thomas Traynell, as we are told in a collection of traditional material published 1720-1731 by the Rev. J Cox and A Holly called *Magna Britannica et Hibernia antiqua et nova* or *A New Survey of Great Britain*, was burnt in Bradford in about 1532 around the same time and for the same reason as a fellow victim at Devizes; both were said to have denied transubstantiation, the doctrine that the bread and wine of the eucharist were literally the body and blood of Christ. This grisly event was doubtless held in the market place at the bottom of modern Market

Street by the bridge foot.

But nationally events were moving rapidly. In 1533 Henry was excommunicated by Pope Clement VII because of his divorce from Catherine of Aragon. Within the next two decades Henry and his successor Edward VI had confiscated all church property, which in Bradford's case meant the Manor of Bradford and the chantries.

St. Catherine's Almshouses, Frome Road.

Of the two Bradford chantries extant in those days the one founded by Thomas Horton (a very rich clothier of whom more later) included a free school and on these grounds the townsfolk pleaded for its continuance. Their pleading partially succeeded. Although the chantry was dissolved, and its property sold to Richard Bellatt and to a nephew of Thomas Horton of the same name, money was made available for William Furbner, the former chantry priest, to continue teaching. (This happened elsewhere also and grammar schools called after Edward VI usually owe their existence to Edward's clemency.)

The other chantry, which seems to have been endowed by the Bird family of Marlborough, had been founded in 1524. William Bird, who was vicar of Bradford, held the appointment of chantry priest as well. He was also chaplain to Lord Hungerford of Heytesbury in respect of the castle at Farleigh Hungerford and this was to prove his undoing. In 1540 Hungerford went to the block on a charge of treason and Bird was likewise accused as his associate. Bird was convicted of using treasonable language against King Henry and was sacked from his living and forfeited the chantry house in which he had lived. Given the character of the man he was being tactless about – among other things he was reported to have called Henry a heretic – he was very lucky indeed not to finish up even more unpleasantly than his patron by being hanged, drawn and quartered, (the prescribed penalty for treason for those not of the peerage). The chantry itself was dissolved about the same time.

3.
EARNING A LIVING

I 'A TRULY NOBLE MANUFACTURE'

All the towne of Bradford stondith by cloth making.
  John Leland (1506-1552)[1]

...the finest medley Spanish cloths, not in England only, but in
the whole world, are made in this part. They told me at
Bradford, That it was no extraordinary thing to have clothiers
worth, from ten thousand to forty thousand pounds a man and
many of the great families, who now pass for gentry in those
counties, have been originally raised from, and built up by this
truly noble manufacture.
  Daniel Defoe (1660-1731)

From the fourteenth century on, promotion of the clothing industry was
the paramount object of England's domestic and foreign policy. Under
King Edward III import of cloth was prohibited, foreign clothworkers
were invited to settle and teach their skills and clothiers were given special
privileges. Later on (1678) a statute required bodies to be buried in cloth
on pain of a substantial fine. Wars were waged to preserve markets overseas. If Old Caspar did not know why Blenheim was such a famous
victory[2] Queen Anne's ministers certainly did. The industry shaped
diplomacy and even served to change national drinking habits. Thus in
1703, the year before Blenheim, Anne's ambassador to Portugal, Bradford-
born John Methuen (c 1650-1706), scion of the rich and powerful clothier
family, negotiated the famous treaty by which English cloth monopolised
the Portuguese market in return for customs preferences for Portuguese
wines over French ones. The cloth monopoly went long ago but the taste
for port and madeira remains.

It was policy which the clothiers of Wiltshire and the Somerset border were well placed to exploit. Good quality wool was to hand. When power was needed fast-flowing rivers drove the mills. The opportunities were vast and they were ably exploited; by John Leland's day the character of Bradford as an important woollen town was already well established and in due course its clothiers would rank among the most powerful in the West Country. From this time on, the story of Bradford until the middle of the last century is largely the story of the clothing industry and its effects, direct and indirect, on town and people.

Fullers, Spinsters, Weavers, Scourers and Dyers

Right up to the eighteenth century the separate processes, from the sheep's back to man's, were, except fulling, hand work. Spinners (invariably female, hence the term spinster) and weavers nearly always worked at home with wheel (or distaff) and loom. So, for that matter, did their employers, the clothiers; which is why former weavers' cottages and clothiers' houses with remains of former workshops attached are so characteristic of Bradford today.

Other processes, scouring, fulling and dyeing called for abundant water and a degree of specialisation. The larger clothiers dyed on their own premises using their own dye-house, the smaller ones shared the facilities of a specialist dyer. The building now called St Margaret's Hall was originally (late eighteenth century) a specialist dyer's dye-house.

Scouring the wool was a stage before weaving, fulling the one immediately after it. Fulling was the process by which the cloth was shrunk and thickened (felted) by beating in water and fuller's earth with stocks (a kind of very large mallet). Water-power was harnessed for this in Bradford on Avon from very early on; one Adam le Folur was employing a powered mill here in 1249 – which makes him Bradford's earliest known industrialist. We happen to know about the Bradford mill because sadly, in that year, Adam's son John was found torn to pieces under the mill-wheel. (The verdict of the Court of Crown Pleas at the inquest was death by misadventure, nobody being suspected; but under the curious law of *deodand* (forfeiture to God) then in force the mill-wheel, as the instrument which had brought about the death, was declared forfeit, its value two shillings.[3]

Adam will also have needed running water for washing the wool and perhaps the woven cloth as well after its natural oil had all been removed by 'scouring' – soaking in human urine. From the down-river side of Bradford town bridge may still be seen the remains of a little artificial island from which scoured wool used to be washed by hand in the stream as late as the latter part of the last century. Adam the Fuller probably had one just like it.

The old dye-house, now St. Margaret's Hall.

Bad Times and Good Ones

The industry had its ups and downs. The first half of the seventeenth century brought very hard times. An inept (and corrupt) government intervention in foreign trade in 1614 (the so-called Cockayne Experiment) sparked retaliation from the Dutch and in the trade war which followed our side got the worst of it. The market for Bradford's chief product, white broad-cloth, declined sharply while the demand for Dutch cloth grew. The slump lasted the better part of the next half century. Resentment and unrest found popular expression when in 1630 a commissioner of Charles I, Anthony Wither, came to investigate complaints about the quality of Bradford cloth; they threw him in the river. In 1632 the town was too impoverished even to keep the town bridge in repair. To make bad matters worse the town was afflicted by plague, once in 1609 and again in 1646.

It was not until after the Civil War (1642-1648)) that things began to mend. The cloth that the Dutch were doing so well with was a high quality product made from Spanish wool. There were technical problems with spinning and weaving Spanish wool which the Dutch had solved but the English had not. Then, in the 1650s, internationally-minded Paul Methuen (died 1667) brought in a Dutch spinner to teach his workers the special know-how. The plan seems to have succeeded. In 1673/4 Trowbridge clothier William Brewer brought in thirty-three more and three of them settled in Bradford; the house called Dutch Barton in Church Street is a reminder of this, though strictly speaking Dutch Barton, so Canon Jones tells us, was the yard of Abbey House (Thomas Horton's house in Leland's day), a short way away.[4]

In sharp contrast to the state of affairs in the first half of the century the second half was, thanks to the enterprise of such as Paul Methuen, a time of prosperity and expansion. The town grew on both sides of the river. There was new building on St Margaret's Hill and on the northern slope where hitherto elderberries had been cultivated (and where perhaps the vineyard recorded in Domesday Book had been located). Newtown was created, then Middle Rank and building began at the east end of Tory. Presbyterians, thanks to the Toleration Act of 1689 now, with all other Protestants, free to worship as they wished, built themselves the Grove Meeting House (now the Zion Baptist Chapel).

Scribbling Engines, Spinning Jennies and Gig Mills[5]
Bad times did not affect master and man alike because the former were better placed to cushion themselves against them by careful investment, usually in land property, in the good times, and in any case to transfer to the work force much of the misery of the bad ones. Moreover, the thrust of the eighteenth century was invention and innovation; and the machines which the masters brought in enriched them and put most of their workers on the parish. Extreme resentment led to mob violence. There was a particularly ugly incident in 1791 when Joseph Phelps, who lived on the job in what is now Westbury House, with his factory behind, in what is now a car park, besieged by a threatening mob of workless, fired on them and killed three. This aspect of the town's history is dealt with more fully in Chapter 9.

However much they might be resisted, the new scribbling engines (for preparing the wool for spinning), the spinning-jenny and spinning-mule,

Opposite: Abbey Mill, built as a cloth mill in 1875, now used for rubber manu-
facture.
Above: Greenland Upper Mill, whose closure in 1905 marked the demise of
Bradford's woollen industry.

the gig-mill (for raising the nap) and the shearing frame, could not be disinvented. They were available and they were profitable to use. They did not need a large, often recalcitrant, labour force but could be run with horse or water-power and later (when coal was readily available from the Somerset coal-fields via the Kennet and Avon Canal), by steam engine. And more and more they took work out of the cottage and on to the factory floor where it was more easily organised, controlled and supervised.

By the end of the century water power was being harnessed for most operations. In 1800 John Jones of Bradford erected at Staverton a grand water mill which a German visitor T A Nemnich described as 'filled with every sort of newly invented machinery so that every kind of process except weaving can be done there.'[6]

Thereafter low wages for those fortunate enough to be in work (and starvation for those who were not) created bitter resentment and sometimes outbreaks of violence. From Bradford in 1802 went a letter to parliament from 'A Souldier Returned to his Wife and weeping Orphans' bitterly complaining about the machinery with the workhouse 'full of lurking boys' because of it; and that though setting fire to property was not right 'Starvation forces Nature to do that which he would not.'[7]

Decline and Fall

After Waterloo there was a steep fall in wages, rents and property prices throughout the country. As time went on things in Bradford went from bad to worse. In 1821 four weavers committed suicide in one day. In 1826 William Cobbett reported (in *Rural Rides*) that he had seen laid-off weavers and spinners from Bradford and elsewhere hand-digging a twelve-acre field because wages had been forced so low that for the farmer it was 'as cheap as ploughing and four times as good.' At Heytesbury he was so moved by the plight of six men and two boys who had walked there from Bradford to get nuts that he went without his own supper and breakfast to give them a proper meal 'for once in their lives.' In 1815 there had been thirty manufacturers who produced in all 678 ends of broadcloth; in 1838 three manufacturers produced 144 ends. In 1840, of the 367 handlooms still in the town every second one was idle. It helped no-one when in the following year one of the local banks failed, partly from indifferent management and partly because of the slump.

By 1867 only two mills remained active, Greenland Upper Mill and one at the Bullpit. In 1875 a new building, Abbey Mill[8], was erected in Church Street but optimism proved misplaced. By 1902 it had closed and it remained empty until 1915 when it was taken over for rubber manufacture. In 1903 the last dye-house (now St Margaret's Hall) closed and in 1905 the last factory, Greenland Upper Mill, did likewise. The seven-centuries old Bradford clothing industry was dead.

II BOUNCING BACK

In 1841, with all but a few looms idle and the failure of local bankers Hobhouse, Phillott and Lowder the outlook was bleak. But things were about to improve, though salvation came from an unexpected quarter.

It was in 1841 that an American called Charles Goodyear (1800-60) discovered how to process rubber in such a way as to make it less susceptible to the action of solvents and changes in temperature and improve its elasticity; in other words to retard 'perishing' and render it more versatile. Among Goodyear's acquaintances was an Englishman, a New York broker called Stephen Moulton (1794-1880). Failing to interest American manufacturers, Goodyear asked Moulton to approach the Macintosh company or some other British manufacturer. Charles Macintosh (1766-1843) was a Glasgow chemical manufacturer who had, since 1824, been treating fabric with rubber solution to make waterproof garments ('macintoshes').

Examining the samples of Goodyear's product which Moulton took to England with him in 1842 Thomas Hancock (1786-1865), Macintosh's partner, also a chemist, concluded that if Goodyear could do it he could too; and he set to work and did. He and Macintosh obtained British patents in 1843, forestalling Goodyear here. At the suggestion of Hancock's friend Brockedon they called the process vulcanization.

Convinced that rubber spelt profitable business, Stephen Moulton returned to England to set up in it himself. Bradford's deserted woollen mills on the banks of the Avon with its clean running water offered him just what he needed. In 1848 he bought Kingston House together with the adjacent Kingston Mill, both semi-derelict, and some other smaller deserted mills near by. Steam-engines and water-wheels were already

Stephen Moulton (1794-1880) founding father of Bradford's rubber industry.

installed and in working order and Moulton was to use both for many years until they were superseded by electricity, itself at first generated on the spot by steam engine and turbine. About this time a friend of Moulton's, Captain Septimus Palairet, who had recently married an American heiress and retired from the army, came to live at Woolley Grange (see later). Palairet also foresaw a bright future for rubber and put up £5,000 to help get things going.

The venture was timely and went well from the start. The new vulcanization technology was put to good and profitable effect to manufacture waterproof clothing for our troops in the Crimea; and new railways throughout the world proved a splendid outlet for hoses for braking and heating and the rubber springs for rolling stock which George Spencer and Co. had patented in 1852 and which Moulton manufactured under licence from them.

George Spencer, Moulton Ltd.

In 1891 George Spencer and the Moulton brothers Horatio and John, Stephen's sons, floated George Spencer, Moulton Ltd. and in due course took over more abandoned cloth factories, including, in 1915, the Church Street and Abbey Mills. By this time waterproof clothing manufacture was long over but the company continued to be world-renowned for design, development and manufacture of products for railways. As time went on automobile and aircraft products were added to the range; also tennis balls. In 1919 a new factory was erected on the site of the Lamb Inn which had stood in the old market place at the northern end of the town bridge.

Avon Industrial Polymers

In 1956 George Spencer, Moulton and Co. became part of the much larger Avon Rubber Company, with its many subsidiary companies in Britain and overseas, and was renamed Avon Industrial Polymers. For another 36 years production continued at Bradford on Avon of buffers, drawgear and suspension components for high-speed 125 Intercity trains, plus, for the automobile industry, windscreen wipers, windscreen seals and engine mountings. For the oil industry the company manufactured in Bradford on Avon a device for use on offshore oil platforms designed to overcome the problem of encrustation by barnacles and seaweed. Also important has been the production of aerosol gaskets and cup seals used in virtually every aerosol manufactured world-wide; seven billion of these have left the works every year.

Avon Industrial Polymers ceased production at Bradford in 1992, of all except aerosol gaskets and cup seals, manufacture of which continues at Abbey Mill in Church Street.

III INDUSTRIES OLD AND NEW

Stone Quarrying

Quarrying for the Cotswold Limestone (jurassic oolite) so readily available is undoubtedly Bradford's oldest continuing industrial activity. The stone produced today (at Westwood) is used mainly for repair and restoration work. Cotswold Limestone is easily sawn and worked but extremely durable; the Saxon church, the town's oldest building, will have been built of stone quarried almost on the spot.

The stone tiles traditionally used for roofing are of forest marble, a much harder stone. Forest marble forms the bedrock at Budbury. The 1841 tithe map (item 1806) shows a tile quarry near Midford. Newly quarried forest marble was left in the open for winter frosts to split it into layers. The mason would then get to work with hammer and chisel. He had a special tool to make a hole in each tile for securing it to the roof, on to which it would be hung with bits of chicken bone or a wooden peg.

Bradford stands on the very edge of the belt of Great and Inferior Oolite which runs in a winding strip from Dorset to Yorkshire; to the east of the town is Cornbrash and Oxford Clay.

Malting and Brewing

Beer has been the Englishman's tipple from time out of mind. Right up to the middle of the last century Bradford's inns and ale-houses brewed their own beer and sometimes made their own malt as well. We know, for example, that Richard Pearce, the eighteenth century Bradford Methodist who kept the Maidenhead Inn (now the Town Club) in Market Street had his own malthouse behind the pub. But malting was a specialist craft, needing space under cover for sprouting the grain and a kiln for processing it and most publicans were content to leave it to the professionals.

In the heyday of the clothing industry small malthouses proliferated, serving the numerous public houses. In 1841, though the industry was in serious decline, there were still nineteen public houses and four malthouses. The malthouse which operated in Frome Road (1841 tithe map item 789) which was then owned by George and Thomas Spencer is commemorated in the name of the flats there, The Maltings. Of the other specialist malthouses shown on the map, one (item 550) was run by William Coles, the ironfounder (see below) at his premises off Trowbridge Road, another (item 580) owned by Richard and John Bethel and run by Richard Blackmore was on the south-west side of Trowbridge Road (Poulton) and the fourth was in Church Street (item 180 – *house and malthouse*) adjacent to Trinity Church Hall.

In 1842, bad times notwithstanding, Alexander Wilkins, a member of the family who ran the nearby Seven Stars Inn (now a private house) where hitherto they had malted and brewed on a small scale for their own pub, erected in Newtown the fortress-like edifice known as the Seven Stars Maltings and Brewery. Malting and brewing continued there up to the First World War. Thereafter the building had various uses until its latest adaptation as residential accommodation.

Small-Scale Engineering

Until the early 1800s such engineering skills as were needed by the farm or the mill were to be found in the blacksmith's forge or at the carpenter's bench. But times were changing. By 1822 John and Job Wastfield were established as makers of water-wheels and shearing frames and William Coles was running a foundry behind his house in Trowbridge Road; it stood near where Blackwell's now is. (He also ran a malthouse there, see above). As time went on the demand for agricultural machinery grew and after about 1850 when George Milsom took over Coles's iron foundry, he added brass founding and agricultural engineering. About the same time his brother Charles, millwright and engineer, had works 'near the bridge'.

The Moulton rubber development created even more demand for local engineering enterprise. S J Brierley (Wilts) Ltd.,'mechanical engineers, millwrights and merchants' operated at 87 Trowbridge Road mainly for the rubber works and we find Berkley Uncles, Milsom's former apprentice, who took over from him in 1899, doing likewise. Uncles manufac-

39

tured mouldings and castings to order; drain and manhole covers bearing the name are still in use in the town. Other foundries were run by H Crisp (Avonside Iron Foundry) located in Bridge Street behind what is now the public library and H Martin, whose workshop was at number 24 Bridge Street in the building until recently called The Old Forge. Among other things Martin cast grave markers; specimens of this work may be seen in the Holt Road cemetery.

Printing and Publishing

The town has never been without a successful printing and publishing enterprise since 1816, when Joseph Rawling (1792-1866) set up first in Market Street, then in Church Street, then again in Market Street (11 and 12), where the business continued into the 1890s. From the 1890s William Charles Dotesio had a press at 17 Silver Street, which continued there till 1934, then moved to Greenland Mills. Dotesios left for Trowbridge in the late 1980s. Today the town's printing and publishing tradition is carried on by Ex Libris Press, established in 1982 by Roger Jones of Ex Libris Bookshop in The Shambles, publishing books of West Country interest.

Mushroom-growing

Bradford's largest stone quarries were underground. Such spent underground quarries, with their stable humidity and even temperatures (average natural temperature 52 to 54 degrees Fahrenheit) are ideal for growing mushrooms. For more than a century mushroom-growing was a major Bradford industry with up to fourteen acres under production.

The industry began in the 1870s, when a Mr Robinson grew mushrooms in Bethell Quarry for making into ketchup. In 1921 Agaric Ltd. set up here; they had been in the business since 1914, first in Surrey, then from 1919 at Corsham. France was the first country to adopt underground cultivation and from the beginning Agaric used French methods; in Bradford they employed French experts. (One of these was Monsieur C Baumann; he settled in the town and descendants of his still live here.) In 1970 Agaric became W Darlington and Sons Ltd, a member of the H J Heinz group of companies. But since modern methods of production favour growing in controlled conditions above ground, in 1992 Darlington abandoned the Bradford on Avon quarries and left the town. Mushroom growing by another firm continues, but on a much smaller scale.

Moulton Developments Ltd.

A small but successful engineering business is carried on by this company. It manufactures the latest version of the small-wheel Moulton bicycle introduced in 1962 by Alex Moulton (great-grandson of Stephen Moulton, founder of the Bradford rubber industry) which in 1964 received the Design Centre Award. Production of that particular model was taken over by the Raleigh Company in 1967 and discontinued in 1974. The current model is the very Rolls Royce of small-wheel pedal bicycles, hand-crafted for excellence and possessing the unusual characteristic that the frame can be dismantled for easy stowage in a matter of seconds. Annual output is some thousand machines, created in a small workshop in the grounds of the Hall. Some dozen workers are employed.

Trio Plastic Products Ltd.

This company was established in 1975 for the manufacture of glassfibre reinforced plastic products to the firm's own design (for example modular insulated cabins, tanks and glassfibre planters) or to customers' specific requirements (for example automobile body panels, machine guards and building cladding panels). There are about sixteen employees.

From the very old to the very new

Two relative newcomers, MPC Data Ltd and Anthony Best Dynamics Ltd, have brought Bradford's industries well into the late twentieth century and seem likely to take them into the twenty first.

MPC Data Ltd

Gas made from coal came to the town in 1834 and until the 1960s it was made from coal at the gasworks in Frome Road. Thereafter most of the site was cleared. The building which had been a warehouse remained, but became derelict. It remained uncared for until 1990, when MPC Data Ltd acquired it, restored it, (TAM Developments of Trowbridge, architect Michael Tollit) and adapted it to their ultra-modern purposes as a computer softward centre.

MPC Data Ltd produce computer programs to order for a wide range of technology-based companies. Their customers include such well-known national and international companies as Hitachi, Sony, Texas Instruments and British Aerospace.

Anthony Best Dynamics Ltd

Located in Holt Road, this company was established in 1982 to offer a computer program service in consultancy, design and development, with particular expertise in noise, vibration and engineering dynamics. They offer a wide range of computer software programmed to solve problems of noise and vibration in anything from private motor vehicles to factory buildings.

Snuff, Twine and even a Windmill

Tobacco was widely grown in Wiltshire in the seventeenth century. At Devizes the firm of Anstie Ltd. was in the snuff and tobacco business until 1960. In the eighteenth century years of depression a Bradford cloth mill went over to producing snuff but the venture was shortlived. It hardly seems enough to justify the epithet 'snuffy' sometimes applied to Bradfordians!

At one time twine was made in Newtown. In the 1970s Mr F King, who had lived in Bradford for 82 years, recalled that when he was at the primary school (which stood where the Rope Walk flats now stand) he would see men at work in what he called the twine yards. Making twine in those days was clearly highly labour-intensive; Mr King described the men 'walking backwards with the hemp all round their waist' while a wheel revolved to spin the twine.

Another short-lived enterprise was Thomas Smart's tower windmill, which, in the early 1800s, he erected just off Mason's Lane on land bought not long before from Thomas Edwards the Elder. Smart was a baker who thought to turn his hand to milling and in 1808 was advertising for help. The scheme was clearly a mistake. The next we hear of the building is that it has become a private house and that Thomas Smart is living in it. The mill is today a guest-house.

Thomas Smart's tower windmill, now called The Round House.

IV CANAL AND RAILWAY

A canal to link the Kennet Navigation at Newbury with the Avon Navigation at Bath to provide a waterway between Bristol and London was authorised by Parliament in 1794. The work was begun in October that year (starting, incidentally, at Bradford) and was complete by 1810.

Bradford was an important port of call and had two wharves, one above the lock and one below it. Trade was brisk. Barges carried goods of every description to and from Bath, Bristol and London and passenger vessels travelled daily between those destinations; Murhill Quarry had its own quarry wharf. Coal from the Somerset coal fields, brought by way of the Somerset Coal Canal which joined the Kennet and Avon at Limpley Stoke, fed the nearby gasworks when gaslighting was brought to the town in the 1830s.

But the canal's era of prosperity was soon over. With the coming of the Great Western Railway in mid-century the canal company were out-rivalled and in 1852 they found themselves obliged to sell to the railway company. The canal nevertheless remained navigable and continued in use until the 1950s. Thereafter it was deserted and rapidly became overgrown along much of its length. Since then, however, the Kennet and Avon Canal Trust, in cooperation with the British Waterways Board, has restored it and it is now open again. At Bradford there is a marina for a hundred leisure craft.

By 1848 the Wilts, Somerset and Weymouth Railway Company, which had been formed in 1844 to create a rail link between Weymouth and Bathampton, had built railway stations at Bradford and Trowbridge. In the same year a line between Chippenham and Trowbridge was opened. But to the dismay of Bradfordians, for the next nine years their station stood in the middle of a field unconnected to anything. Money had run out and investors had become chary. Among other things the length to Bathampton had proved more expensive than had been envisaged. The construction of seven viaducts and more especially two aqueducts, one to carry the Kennet and Avon canal over the line at Avoncliff and the other to do the same at Limpley Stoke had posed engineering problems. At Avoncliff, burrowing under the canal put it out of commission for a while and there were major problems with the creation of the Dundas aqueduct at Limpley Stoke – 'a tedious and rather difficult operation'

Above: Bradford Wharf on the Kennet and Avon Canal, for many years out of use, now once again in business, though only for pleasure. With the coming of the Great Western Railway the canal, outmoded, went into decline.
Below: Bradford on Avon Railway Station, built in 1848 but not brought into use until 1857.

Brunel called it. In 1850 the WSWR company went into liquidation and its assets were taken over by the Great Western Railway.

In 1857, at long last, the line through Bradford was finished and passed inspection; and on the 2nd February, by way of celebration, a free special left Bradford station for Weymouth.

NOTES

1. John Leland (*c* 1506-1552), chaplain to Henry VIII and his Library Keeper, was appointed King's Antiquary in 1533 and commissioned to search ecclesiastical establishments throughout the country for records and manuscripts. Between 1536 and 1542 he toured the whole of England. Besides his main purpose he made notes on the places he visited. In 1540 he visited Bradford and much of what we know about what the town was like then we owe to these notes.

Leland intended his researches to be the basis of a great work on *The History and Antiquities of the Nation* but did not live to accomplish it. He lost his reason in 1550 and died two years later. *Leland's Itinerary* was published in nine volumes in 1710 and *Collectanea* in six volumes in 1715.

2. I refer to John Southey's ironic lines:
    "And everybody praised the Duke,
    Who this great fight did win."
    "But what good came of it at last?"
    Quoth little Peterkin.
    "Why that I cannot tell" said he
    "But 'twas a famous victory."
The Battle of Blenheim in 1704 took place in the course of the War of the Spanish Succession (1702-13). At Blenheim, on the River Danube in Germany, the English army under the Duke of Marlborough destroyed the French one. As a result of this and other setbacks King Louis XIV of France was rendered powerless to close Spain – and therefore South America and the Mediterranean – to English cloth. Gibraltar was seized at the same time and for the same reason.

3. A similar accident happened at Avoncliff in the same year but in this instance the owner was a miller, William by name. The victim was a youth called David.

4. Article in *Wiltshire Archaeological Magazine* Vol. XX page 306.

5. The gig mill replaced 'teasing' (raising the nap) by hand. Both methods used the head of the teasel (*dipsacus fullonum*) fixed in a frame called a 'handle'. The cloth was damped for teasing and handles needed to be dried after use. 'Handle-houses' were used for this.

6. Quoted by K G Ponting in *Wool and Water*. The building, minus four of its original six storeys, but still impressive, belongs now to the Nestle Co.

7. E P Thompson: *The Making of the Working Class* quoting Hammond: *The Skilled Labourer*.

8. This excellent building was designed by a leading London architect, Richard Gane. In 1971 it was restored by Avon Industrial Polymers Ltd.

4 CHURCHES, CHAPELS AND MEETING HOUSES

I PARISH CHURCHES

The Saxon Church

With the coming of the Normans, and the building by them near by of a grander church, the one built by the Saxons will have fallen gradually into disuse. We hear of it again in 1614 when Gifford Yerbury is stated to have held a 'chappell' and other property by copyhold from the lord of the manor. What the old Saxon church was used for during the next hundred years we do not know but in 1715 we find it being called variously the 'skull-house' and 'the bone-house', which suggests that it had become, in part at least, an ossuary. In 1712 the rector of the day, John Rogers, established there a free school for boys of Bradford parish. We know from the Charity Commissioners' report of 1834 that the premises then comprised 'an underground cellar, two rooms and garret above stairs, one room and a small pantry below, a large school room, kitchen underneath, a recess adjoining, commonly called the bone-house, and a small place attached to the school-house for the convenience of the boys.' The report commented that the whole building was in a very dilapidated state.

In about 1856 repair work happened to uncover carvings in stone of two angels over what we now know was the original chancel arch. Thus alerted, the archaeologically-minded vicar of Holy Trinity, Canon W H R Jones, discovered, submerged in the accretions of the centuries, the outlines of the nave and chancel of a small church. A few years later J T Irvine, an architect well known for his distinguished work on Bath Abbey and other important buildings also began to take an interest in it. It was, however, still in part the charity school in the hands of trustees and in part a separate cottage in private hands, so it was not yet possible to consider restoration. But from 1869 Irvine did a number of sketches which, together with his notes, form an excellent record of the building as it was before restoration and at the various stages in its rehabilitation. (These notes and drawings are in Bath reference library.) Then one day in 1871, Canon Jones, browsing in the Bodleian library at Oxford, came upon a recently-published book containing the text of the *Gesta Pontificum* of William of Malmesbury. The following passage caught his eye:

> *Et est ad hunc diem eo loco ecclesiola quam ad nomen beatissima Laurentii fecisse predicatur Aldhelmus.*

> At that place [*viz* Bradford] there is to this day a little church which Aldhelm is said to have built to the name of the most blessed Laurence.

The words had been written about the year 1125. Here was clear confirmation of the church's considerable antiquity and evidence (admittedly hearsay) that it was even older than had hitherto been supposed, though Jones, in a letter to Irvine, was cautious enough to comment only that the passage carried back the little church 'to the beginning of the twelfth century at all events'. He also reported that he had succeeded in purchasing the chancel (hitherto occupied as a cottage) and a plot of ground all round sufficient to isolate it within boundary walls.

Thereafter there was steady progress. A trust was formed (the first trustees were, besides Jones, Lord Nelson, Sir John Awdry, Sir Charles Hobhouse, J H Parker and the Rev. E L Barnwell) and fund-raising begun. In June 1874 the trustees were in full possession of the entire building, having exchanged it for Old Church House (now called Trinity Church Hall), a few yards down the street, to which the school was then transferred. Irvine was appointed architect for the restoration; but Canon Jones, in his enthusiasm to press on with the work, brought in a local architect also. Work was done of which Irvine disapproved as out of keeping. In 1881 he resigned specifically over the trustees' instructions that the master's house should be demolished and replaced with buttresses.

The Church of the Holy Trinity

If the monastery which the Danes destroyed in about 1015 was indeed built by Aldhelm when he became abbot of Malmesbury in the year 675;

The Saxon Church of St. Lawrence

Above: Saxon stone carvings on the chancel arch.
Below: Blind arcading on the east wall. The pilasters
are characteristic of late Saxon work.

and if, as seems possible, the original Saxon Church building was built alongside about the same time, then the area where the parish church of the Holy Trinity stands has been hallowed by Christian worship for over thirteen hundred years.

The Church of the Holy Trinity is usually dated back to about 1150 on the basis that the little church that William of Malmesbury was writing about in 1125 was the only one in the parish. But we know that William the Conqueror was a dedicated ecclesiastical reformer and that by the time of his death in 1087 all the Saxon bishops had been replaced by Norman ones and Saxon church buildings were being replaced or rebuilt in the Romanesque (or Norman) style. The very fact that a Saxon church was there to be snubbed argues for an earlier date; and William of Malmesbury does call the Saxon church by the diminutive *ecclesiola* - as if it were not the principal one. So Holy Trinity *could* be older than mid-twelfth century.

What we see today from the outside is not so very different from what a twelfth century Bradfordian would have seen. The Normans built a nave, a chancel and a tower. The chancel was lengthened about a century later. The tower is different; the present one was probably erected in the fifteenth century. The building is wider; in about the fifteenth century the north wall was pierced and arched and the nave extended to create what is now an aisle but which in pre-Reformation days will have formed the Hall, Bird and Horton chantry chapels mentioned earlier. On the south side is an extension, now used as the sacristy but built as a chapel in about the sixteenth century, possibly by a member of the Hall family. Our twelfth century Bradfordian would recognise the window over the south door and the round-headed windows of the chancel, but none of the others.

Over the years the interior of the building has suffered at the hands of reformers. Preserved at the west end of the nave is all that remains of the pre-Reformation painted rood screen, showing two figures with a manuscript with verses from the opening chapter of St John's gospel; the rest of the screen will have been torn down at the time of the Reformation.

When Canon Jones was appointed to the living in 1851 he was a little dismayed by what he found. As a result of his efforts major works of repair and restoration were carried out in 1864-66. The work was completed and the church re-opened on 13 February 1866. Some idea of how the building had been neglected is given by the report of the occasion in the

Hallowed by Christian worship for over 1,300 years? Here, where Bishop Aldhelm's monastery probably once stood, stand side by side the Saxon and Norman churches and the chantry house (seen to the right of the church tower). On the skyline is the chapel of St. Mary, Tory.

Trowbridge Advertiser on 17 February 1866. It was described as having been 'in a most dilapidated state, the walls being out of perpendicular and the arches and columns in such a state as to render it unsafe to assemble in for public worship'. Unsightly galleries had been removed. 'Pews of all heights and dimensions, many of them being so situated as to preclude their occupants from the sight of the minister and the sound of his voice' had been replaced by 'open low seats'.

Discovered in the course of the restoration work was what remained of a full-size thirteenth or fourteenth century stone female effigy; it was found, charming wimpled[1] face down, having been used to repair paving. Because effigies of females of that date are rare it has been conjectured that the lady commemorated was a member of the rich and powerful Hall family, perhaps Agnes, wife of Reginald de Aula who died in 1250. The effigy is at the west end under the remains of the painted rood screen.

Near by is a facsimile of the so-called Bishop's Bible[2] of 1572. The original volume, now safely in the Wiltshire Record Office, was discovered for sale in a Bradford second-hand furniture shop.

Interesting features in the north aisle are the carved stone ornamentation in the north wall, most probably the reredos to the altar of one of the chantry chapels, and the eighteen-foot long squint (perhaps the longest in England), pierced through the original Norman north wall. On the east wall and to the left of the squint is a brass commemorating Thomas Horton (died 1530), the rich Bradford clothier and property-owner, and his wife Mary, prepared in their lifetimes (dates of deaths left to be inserted later but the job never done) with Thomas's merchant's mark – the mark he attached to his bales of cloth – displayed and Thomas clearly as proud of it as any nobleman of his coat of arms. Nearby in the north wall is the stained glass window commemorating Canon W H Jones, vicar, celebrated Bradford historian and antiquary and discoverer, as we have seen, of the long-lost Saxon Church; and next to it, interestingly, one to his contemporary, Joseph Rawling, Methodist minister at Lady Huntingdon's chapel. Rawling died in 1866 and Jones in 1885 so the window evidently had the good canon's approval.

A window on the south wall has stained glass of Flemish origin consisting of a number of roundels depicting scenes from the life of Jesus; this was the gift of John Ferret (1702-70). These roundels are believed to have been based on drawings by the German painter and engraver Albrecht Dürer (1471-1528).

Holy Trinity has a splendid peal of eight bells, the two oldest dated 1614, the most recent 1882, a clock without a dial (but which strikes the quarters as well as the hour) and a carillon. There had been the equivalent of a carillon from 1737, when John Knott installed, for £27, a set of bells 'to play any tune with pleasure in the compass of eight bells'. In 1913 a carillon by Gillett and Johnson of Croydon was installed which plays the tunes of four hymns, 'Holy, Holy, Holy; Jerusalem my Happy Home; God Moves in a Mysterious Way'; and 'The Sicilian Mariners' Hymn.'

We hear first of a new organ in a vestry minute of 1729. It was installed in a gallery at the west end of the church. Edward Orpin was appointed organist at a salary of £15 a year and held the post till his death in 1781. His daughter Elizabeth succeeded him and continued till her death in 1786, although for the last seven or eight years of her life she was blind. At the end of the century the instrument was still in good shape; the 1793 edition of the Universal British Directory entry for Bradford praises it. (This may also be a tribute to the organist of the day, Daniel Mullings, appointed at the age of fourteen in 1791, described in the vestry records as having a 'genius for musick'.) To judge, however, by the heavy repair bills shown in the vestry accounts, the organ was beginning to wear out and when Canon Jones arrived on the scene in 1851 it had been abandoned. The choir was, instead, accompanied by a small amateur orchestra. The major repair work of 1864-66 included restoration of the organ and its removal to what is now the sacristy. The present organ was installed in 1926.

The poor state in which Canon Jones found the church suggests an attitude of indifference on the part of his predecessors. From 1793 to 1799 and again from 1808 to 1835 one of these was royal protégé Frederic William Blomberg.

Blomberg was a natural son of George III by Melissa Layng, who was married to Captain Frederick Blomberg. Blomberg was not only vicar of Bradford on Avon but for most of the time also vicar of Shepton Mallett, a Prebendary of Bristol and also of Westminster, chaplain to George, Prince of Wales, (later George IV), a canon of Westminster up to 1822 and then a canon of St Paul's cathedral. So the parish to him represented only a small part of his income and was neglected. Blomberg left Bradford on Avon to take up the appointment of vicar of St Giles's, Cripplegate, and died there on 23 March 1847.[3]

Christ Church

The juxtaposition of great riches and dire poverty was characteristic of Victorian England. By the middle of the century much of Bradford was badly run down; towards the end of it an official report described the area near the parish church where Trinity Church Hall (then the Free Grammar School) stands as being 'in a bad part of the town', and just across the river from it the British School was closed by the authorities because of its unsavoury surroundings. But high on the hill on the northern outskirts things were very different. Berryfield House (now a hospital) had been built and Frankleigh House, now a private school, had been refurbished on the grand scale. A few years later Captain Palairet re-modelled Woolley Grange, later to become Woolley Grange Hotel. Money in some pockets was plentiful and what better use for it than to build a brand-new church?

Christ Church was, accordingly, commissioned in 1839 and consecrated two years later. It was designed by G P Manners of Bath and erected by Jones Brothers of Bradford. It cost £3,862, raised by public subscription.

A contemporary painting of the interior shows plain glass windows, plain walls and stone-flagged floor. This 'style of rigid simplicity', as Canon Jones called it, was far *too* simple for the taste of Victorian England, and in 1875 the new vicar, Richard Umfraville Lambert (1829-1905), set about remedying matters. The famous church architect Sir Gilbert Scott was engaged and produced the design for the building much as we see it today, chancel added beyond the present communion rail, altar raised, choir stalls created, a new organ installed, gallery removed, all the pews changed for new ones, walls decorated, stained glass introduced and gas-lighting fitted on wrought-iron chandeliers. Almost Scott's last work, Jones commented in the Wiltshire Archaeological Magazine in August 1881, that it was now 'well worth a visit.'

There were further changes after the First World War. The Lady Chapel was added by the Moulton family as a memorial to Eric Moulton, killed in action in France in 1916; and in 1923 the peal of eight bells was given by Brigadier General Palmer of Berryfield House.

The first incumbent was perpetual curate John Hopkins Bradney (died 1861) who lived at Leigh House which he bought in 1840 presumably in anticipation of his appointment the following year.

The parsonage, at 3 Mason's Lane, was acquired by the Ecclesiastical

Commissioners in 1844 and was occupied by the Reverend J C Earle who succeeded Bradney as vicar. It had been built as a private house some time after 1819 by James Budgett.[4]

The old town hall, now the Roman Catholic Church of St. Thomas More.

The Roman Catholic Church of St Thomas More

In 1955, after the lapse of centuries, a Roman Catholic parish once again came into being to serve Bradford, Holt, Monkton Farleigh, Westwood, Winsley, and Wraxall. The church building is the one-time town hall in Market Street, which assumed its latest role on June 25, 1955, when Dr Joseph Rudderham, Bishop of Clifton, gave the inaugural blessing.

The building was exactly one hundred years old. In its day it had housed Bradford Urban District Council, a masonic lodge and a cinema. It was designed by Thomas Fuller (1822 - 1898) of Bath[5] and erected by James Long on behalf of a private company for leasing to Bradford Urban District Council. It remained the council offices until 1910, when the owners put it up for sale. The council having refused to buy, it then became the town's first cinema.

II NONCONFORMITY AND DISSENT

Il y a en Angleterre soixante sectes religieuses différentes, et une seule sauce.
In England they have sixty different religious sects but only one sauce.
                                                    (Attributed to Voltaire)

If Queen Elizabeth could spurn the Vatican, her subjects could, at least, disagree with the Church of England. Or so they seemed to think. The Elizabethan establishment would doubtless have preferred all to submit themselves to the established church, and indeed, it was unlawful not to attend. After Elizabeth's death in 1603 English Protestantism seemed at risk, her Stuart successors being Roman Catholics at heart. But towards the century's end the 'Glorious Revolution' (1688) which unseated Rome-inclined James II finally brought to rest the Catholic-Protestant see-saw which Henry VIII had set in motion a century and a half before. By this time Protestant dissenting sects abounded and one of the first actions of the new monarchy of William and Mary was to acknowledge their right to worship in their own way provided their place of worship was formally registered with the local magistrates.

We know from the records of these registrations[6] that in Bradford there have been Baptists, Congregationalists, Independents, Methodists, Presbyterians, Quakers and Unitarians. Today we have the Old Baptist Chapel, the Bearfield Congregational Church, the Quakers (Religious Society of Friends), the United Church and the Zion Baptist Chapel, all with ancestry rooted in the seventeenth century.

The Old Baptist Chapel

The Baptists had secured a strong foothold in England, first in London in 1612, then in the country at large. The Old Baptist Chapel in St Margaret's Street derives its origins from the first-comers from before 1672; in that year they registered John Broome's barn as their place of worship. Seventeen years later they built a chapel to hold three hundred on land off St Margaret's Street belonging to Zachariah Shrapnel. This was rebuilt on the same site in 1797. Like other religious bodies everywhere, the Bradford church has suffered its schisms, the chief of which occurred in 1842, when part of the congregation left to join the Independents at Zion Chapel (see below); and during the first half of the present century the church experienced (in the words of Robert W Oliver in his paper[7]) the most barren period of its long history. But, thanks to the devoted efforts of individuals, the church survived to celebrate its tercentenary and looks set to continue.

The Grove Meeting House

Now called Zion Baptist Chapel, the Grove Meeting House which stands at the eastern end of Middle Rank was erected in 1698 by Presbyterians. Presbyterianism, which had been established in England under Cromwell, was strong in this country until about the middle of the eighteenth century. Thereafter it declined; members seceded in groups or just drifted away, some to become Baptists, others Independents, others Unitarians.

Before they built the Grove Meeting House Bradford Presbyterians had been worshipping from at least 1672 at the house of John Holton; and twenty years later at Francis Yerbury's house or in his barn, both of which places were registered.[8]

The Grove Meeting House (now Zion Baptist Chapel) built in 1698, the oldest nonconformist place of worship in the town.

By 1739 the Grove Meeting House congregation was leaning heavily towards Unitarianism. The minister, Dr Joshua Read, found this not to his liking and with his supporters left (see later). His successor was Dr Roger Flexman (1708-95)[9] from Chard, Presbyterian and Calvinist. In Bradford he married a member of his congregation, Catharine, daughter of clothier John Yerbury (1678-1728).

In January 1793 the Grove Meeting House congregation adopted the Unitarian liturgy, though they still called themselves Presbyterians. Among the leaders were men of good standing in the town, including rich clothiers John William Yerbury and his brother-in-law John Moggridge. But by 1815 the congregation had dwindled to almost nothing and shortly afterwards the building was being used by the Independents who had separated from Morgan Hill (see below). From 1823 Zion Chapel, which they had built on the Conigre across the way, was their place of worship.

In 1842 they were joined by a group who had seceded from the Baptists in St Margaret's Street (see above).Thereafter they called themselves Particular Baptists or Zion Chapel Baptists.

The Grove Meeting House remained in Presbyterian ownership but was used by them only occasionally. In 1876, following Charity Commission investigations, it was vested in the Official Trustee of Charity Lands. From about this time the Zion Baptists rented it as an annex, then in 1939 they closed Zion Chapel and made Grove Meeting House their main place of worship. Zion Baptist Chapel continues at the Grove Meeting House, which not only makes it the oldest nonconformist place of worship in the town but also the only one to be used continuously as such since its erection nearly three centuries ago.

Zion Chapel was demolished in the wave of destruction which afflicted the town in the 1960s.

The United Church, St Margaret's Hill

The Presbyterians who under Dr Joshua Read seceded from the Grove in January 1739 built a new chapel on Morgan Hill (now St Margaret's Hill) on land given by Sarah Grant (died 1741) of Bradford. Walter Grant of Monkton Farleigh, Sarah's brother, John Pitman of Bradford and Joshua Read himself each gave £100. The chapel opened in 1741 and was registered as Independent.

The stone tablet on the front of the building records that it was built as an Independent Meeting in 1740 and enlarged in 1798 and 1835.

In 1815 disagreement with the trustees about their powers in relation to the pastor led to a split and the dissidents left and took over the Grove, as stated above. Attempts at reconciliation failed, but were not totally fruitless; the trustees relinquished the powers which had started the row. Today the church is the forward-looking and ecumenically-minded United Church, comprising the United Reformed and Methodist Churches, with antecedents including Congregational and English Presbyterian churches.

Bearfield Congregational Church

This congregation maintains its long tradition of independence.

The building was erected in 1787 as Bethel Chapel. It was registered as Independent, the property of Caleb Hodges 'and others'. The liturgy was Anglican. After only a few years it closed. The history of the present persuasion begins with its purchase by the Reverend Thomas Watkins of Bath. Watkins died in 1802 and left the chapel to his widow, who in 1806 married Joseph Rawling, a schoolmaster and preacher from Ide in Devon. Rawling was in pastoral charge till his death in 1816. Not long after this the chapel was taken over by Lady Huntingdon's Connexion (originally upper-crust Methodist-become-Calvinist[10] and from 1790 separated from Wesleyan Methodism). Its memory lingers in Bradford in the name of the street where it was located, but its impact here was slight, its congregation not at all what Lady Huntingdon had in mind.

When Joseph Rawling (1792-1866) grandson of the Joseph Rawling who had been minister up to 1816 agreed in 1847 to take charge (without stipend) he did so partly because he was sorry for the far from well-off members, seven in all, in their dilapidated chapel, and partly in his grandfather's memory. He thought of it as deserting Methodism and regretted leaving the chapel on Coppice Hill of which he had been steward since it opened in 1818. But as things turned out he was able to preserve links and later on we find him preaching at Coppice Hill and at Zion Chapel, too, on occasion.

Rawling made the chapel the love of his life. In 1849 overdue repairs were carried out and shortly afterwards he installed an organ. The congregation was never large, but it did survive. Fourteen years after his death it became Congregationalist, a natural step given its Calvinist antecedents, though for many years it was still known as Lady Huntingdon's Chapel.

Providence Baptist Chapel, Bearfield

This chapel was opened in 1858. Its congregation was never large, and, having long ceased to be a place of worship, the building is now residential.

Methodism

On Tuesday 17 July 1739 John Wesley rode into Bradford from Bath for the first of many visits. He had looked forward to fruitful co-operation with Joshua Read, the Presbyterian minister whom he had met in Bath, and in his journal he records his disappointment at being rebuffed by him. What he will not have known at the time was that, as we have seen, Read had recently left the Grove in a huff and must have been under stress. Read was no doubt fearful of the effect Wesley might have on his already diminished flock, particularly since, as he told Wesley, he had heard that he had been regarded at Oxford as a little crack-brained. Moreover, he had, for the time being, no church premises of his own, only John Pitman's house as a place of worship.

Wesley was almost as disappointed with the vicar, John Rogers, who was not willing to make his church available on a week-day, though he declared himself glad of assistance on a Sunday. (Wesley was, of course, an ordained priest of the Anglican communion).

Paradoxically Wesley had better luck with the Quakers. After preaching at Bearfield to an audience of about a thousand he called on Constant Bailward[11], Quaker minister, widow of a rich Quaker clothier, and so began what was to become a lifelong association with the Bailward family.

Wesley was greatly attracted to Bradford and seems to have been exceptionally well received. He preached at Bearfield some half dozen times in the year of his first visit to audiences of (he claimed) up to ten thousand. Over the next fifty years he visited the town on twenty-six occasions.

The first registration of a Methodist place of worship in Wiltshire was at Bradford, in 1756. The licence describes it as 'lately erected adjoining the dwellinghouse of John Silby' and the applicants were 'John Silby and others'. It had been built by Richard Pearce landlord of the Maidenhead Inn in Pippet Street (now Market Street), behind his pub, where a malthouse had been. Pearce had become a leading Methodist.[12] Worship continued at the Pippet Street chapel until 1818 when a much grander building was erected on Coppice Hill. (The old building, now 29 Market Street, today houses the Bradford on Avon Town Club.)

Wesley seems to have disliked the chapel as a place to preach; an entry in the Journal for 18 September 1764 records that 'being determined to be no longer cooped up in the room at Bradford' he moved down to near the bridge (in fact, the market place then) where a 'multitude' flocked to hear him. The following day he again preached for preference in the open, this time at Whitehill where 'many had an opportunity of hearing who would not come to the room.' Preaching in the open had its hazards, though, as the townsfolk were not always friendly. At Whitehill 'the beasts of the people were tolerably quiet' till Wesley had nearly finished his sermon. 'They then lifted up their voice, especially one, called a gentleman, who had filled his pocket with rotten eggs; but a young man coming unawares, clapped his hands on each side and mashed them all at once. In an instant he was perfume all over ...'

Worse had befallen travelling preacher William Hitchens, a dozen years before. He was thrust into the lock-up on the bridge[11] by the press-gang pending compulsory enlistment. Richard Pearce tried unsuccessfully to get him out on bail; the authorities said they would take his word for £10,000 (he must have been pretty well-off) but not for Hitchens. In the event the magistrates had to set Hitchens free when he was able to satisfy them that he owned property and was thus exempt from military service. Though uncomfortable his confinement was for him rewarding; sleepless all night he preached to his guard of twelve soldiers who, as he observed, 'durst not leave.'[13]

On his early visits to Bradford on Avon Wesley sometimes stayed overnight at a boarding-house, now 6 Silver Street. There, he is said to have told his host, the beds were truly English; they had 'no notion of giving out'. (The old building today is egregious for its red brick frontage, perpetrated around the turn of the present century). On later visits Wesley enjoyed private hospitality, whether with staunch Methodist Richard Pearce, at the Maidenhead Inn, Samuel Rayner of Pottick's House (as we know from an entry in The Journal on 12 March 1784) or Anne Bailward, daughter-in-law of Constant. In September 1787 he stayed at Anne Bailward's for the last time. A year later he records her death: 'good Mrs. Bailward ... after long struggling with a deep nervous disorder, which for a time depressed the mind as well as the body, the cloud removed; her load fell off, and her spirit joyfully returned to God.'

The 'blind house' (lock-up) on the town bridge, sometimes called 'the chapel'. The pointed ribbed arch of the bridge is believed to be original (late Norman).

In her will Anne Bailward left £80 for the benefit of the preachers at 'Mr Wesley's Preaching House at Bradford' so long as they preached according to his doctrine.

On 18 September 1789 John Wesley, now eighty-six, preached at the Bradford chapel, for the last time, to the 'old, steady congregation; but many of them gone into a better world. Scarce any of the rich and honourable left; but it is enough that the gospel is preached to the poor.' The following day, however, at Bath, there were 'rich and honourable in abundance ... and seemed as attentive as colliers.' Doubtless his thoughts went back to when, at nearby Kingswood a half century before, he had preached amid the slagheaps to the coalminers – and evangelical Methodism was born.

In the forty years after Wesley's death in 1791 Methodism throve in Bradford as it did elsewhere. Nationwide, numbers went from 72,000 to 237,000. In Bradford the congregation outgrew the Pippet Street chapel and in 1818 a splendid new one was erected on Coppice Hill. Joseph Rawling, the Congregationalist minister, tells us in his autobiography (see above) that 'in those days the rich and influential among the inhabitants of Bradford and vicinity did not consider themselves out of place or lowering their position to attend a Wesleyan ministry.' Among these he numbered the Cams of Chantry House and John Smith, local attorney, whose daughter married (in 1805) distinguished churchman Dr Thomas Coke (1747-1814).[15]

Before the end of the last century Bradford ceased to be a leading centre and the decline continued in the present one. By the 1950s the congregation was not large enough to maintain the chapel and had to give up using it. In 1974 they crossed the town to join the United Reformed Church at St Margaret's Hill. The old chapel on Coppice Hill, now roofless, was sold to an adjoining owner who turned it into a private open-air swimming pool.

Two of Wesley's Bradford preachers achieved more than purely local renown in the church. Adam Clark was only here for one year, sent in 1782 by Wesley himself at the age of twenty. The young Irishman was, like Wesley, a brilliant, convincing and indefatigable speaker. Clearly a young man in a hurry, in his comparatively brief stay he preached over five hundred sermons and married a Trowbridge girl, Mary Cooke. He then went off to a life of service to the movement acting several times as president of the Methodist Conference and achieving distinction as the author of a Bible commentary.

Quite different was Thomas Olivers (1725-1799) who was in Bradford from 1749-53, in which time he went from convert to, from 1751, local preacher. Olivers was born at Tregynon, Montgomeryshire. His parents both died when he was a small boy and so did an uncle who cared for him after their death. At the age of eighteen he was apprenticed to a shoemaker. He was self-educated – 'a rough stick of wood' Wesley called him – who as well as working in paid employment six days a week, dedicated the whole of Sunday, apart from two to three hours sleep from about 2 am, to his ministry. He would cover over twenty miles on foot in the course of visiting 'a few poor people' from 6 – 7.00 am, preaching at different places at 1.00 pm and 5.00 pm then walking home so tired that he could scarce get over a stile or upstairs to bed.

In his spare time he wrote hymns, at least one of which 'The God of Abraham' praise remains highly regarded. He is said to have translated it from the Hebrew, giving it, as far as he could, a Christian character, and to have used for tune a synagogue melody furnished by a Jewish friend Leoni.

In 1752 there was a serious smallpox epidemic in the town, and Olivers caught the disease and nearly died of it. He was grievously ill from October to New Year's Day, when he got out of bed for the first time to have the sheets changed. (It is clear that personal hygiene was not paramount in mid eighteenth century Bradford on Avon. Olivers had a room in the house of a Mrs Antill, which he described as large and airy, yet Mrs Antill told him that though she only came occasionally into it people told her that her clothes smelt.) Olivers tells how Richard Pearce, 'that pattern of pastoral Christianity' engaged one of the best nurses in town, the chief apothecary and Dr Clark 'the most experienced physician in all that country' to look after him. (John Clark was the Quaker medical practitioner mentioned later.)

About this time Olivers received a small legacy with which, on his recovery, he bought a horse and travelled about paying old debts. Finding on his return to Bradford that he had not enough money to repay Richard Pearce he sold horse and saddle, keeping the saddle-bags so that he could in future be his own pack-horse, only to find that Pearce refused to accept.

In October, packing his books and and other few belongings in the saddle-bags and slinging them across his shoulders, he set off, at Wesley's behest, to preach the word in Cornwall. A well-wisher later gave him a horse which he was still riding twenty-five years later. What a character!

Olivers was buried in John Wesley's tomb at the City Road, London, burying ground.

The Coppice Hill chapel had an outpost at Bradford Leigh from 1822. It was registered as being at the house of James Hibberd, registrant James M Byron, Bradford Methodist minister. In 1892 a mission chapel was erected but it has been closed for many years.

Primitive Methodism

This group of Methodists seceded from the main church in 1810. Its appeal was to the poorest in the community. In 1825 'a building in the occupation of William Brown' was registered as their place of worship; the registrants were John Challinor and William Brown. In 1845 they registered 'the chapel and premises now in the holding and occupation of William Crook, John Smith and others'; this presumably will have been the old chapel now converted to a dwelling-house at Sladesbrook. The church was never a strong one and ceased to exist as a separate body in 1932, when it was reunited with the Methodist Church.

The Quakers

By 1660 the Quakers of Bradford were worshipping regularly (and at that time illegally) just outside the town at Frankleigh – they called it Cumberwell – probably in the home of one of their number. It was in that year that a troop of cavalry broke into their meeting for worship and seized one of them, Robert Starr, whence he was taken to Sarum (Salisbury) and thrown into gaol.[16]

By 1661 they had their own burial ground at Frankleigh and by 1676 owned a meeting house also. The meeting house was rebuilt by 1689 and Frankleigh continued as a place of worship and burial up to the end of the next century; the last burial there was in 1803. In 1813 it was sold for private occupation. It is now 119 Bath Road.

After the Toleration Act of 1689 it was lawful for Quakers and other Protestant dissenters to meet for worship in their own way and in 1718 a second Quaker meeting house was erected, this one in the town centre. It was a substantial building, seating two hundred, and cost £240 to build. With a burial ground[17] adjoining it stood in the area now bounded by St Margaret's Hall, the Riverside Restaurant and the houses in St Margaret's Street.

Between about 1670 and 1730 Bradford Quakers were numerous and influential. Thereafter membership declined and by the end of the eighteenth century both meeting houses were closed, the few remaining members transferring their membership to Melksham Meeting.

The Bailward family were early Bradford Quakers. Constant Bailward (died 1744 and buried at Cumberwell) was a Quaker minister. She was born Constant Owen of Nailsworth and married John Bailward in 1713. Both Constant and John were active in the movement. Quaker minutes record, for example, a meeting for church affairs at their house in July 1729; and travelling Quaker minister Thomas Story recorded in his journal on 6 July 1731 that he stayed with them. Story noted that John, evidently a practising lawyer, was then having difficulties with the authorities, in particular with Judge Ayres, who was refusing to accept John's affirmation in lieu of oath.[18]

Their son John, born 1715, in 1744 married Anne, daughter of Quaker linen draper Thomas Shewell of London.[19] But as time went on John and Anne drifted away from the Society of Friends. Anne seems to have hovered between Wesleyan Methodism (as we have seen) and the Anglican Church. In July 1780 she and her husband were recorded as having 'seat rooms in the pews' of the parish church[20] (though the entry is crossed through); and a mural tablet in the parish church records Anne's death (on 25 July 1788) at the age of 75. John was a trustee of the Methodist chapel. Their son Samuel married Anna Maria Stevens, a Methuen heiress and the Bailwards joined the ranks of the landed gentry, in due course to be celebrated as such in Burke's distinguished volumes.

The local doctor and surgeon in the late seventeenth / early eighteenth century, John Clark, (died 1726) was a Quaker. His two sons, John (1684-1760) and William, were also medical practitioners and also active Quakers. They will have learnt their profession as apprentices, probably of their father. John succeeded his father in the practice; this was the Dr Clark who attended Thomas Olivers the Methodist preacher when he had smallpox. William, after spending some years from 1718 in Ireland, returned for a while to Bradford on Avon, then, some time before 1728, left for London.[21]

The elder John Clark had started life as a cabinet-maker in London; the events leading to his somewhat startling metamorphosis as a medical man are not on record. Perhaps it was that he found he had the gift of healing. He was clearly no charlatan and was held in high esteem by his fellow Quakers, for many years holding the position of clerk (chairman) of the group of Wiltshire meetings of which Bradford and Cumberwell (Frankleigh) were constituent members. His wife Anne (died 1745) was a minister, contemporary with Constant Bailward.

Some family names recur frequently in the early Quaker records. Examples are Baskerville (John, clothier, lived in Newtown, married Ann Webb also of Bradford in 1701), Grant (George, clothier, 1698), Moxham (John, died 1733), Noyes (Israel, clothier, 1723), Tyler (Charles of Bearfield, clothier, married Sarah Sanger in 1734). The Knees of Trowbridge were members of the Bradford Meeting in the late eighteenth century.

A Quaker Meeting re-opened in Bradford in 1971 after a lapse of over 170 years. The old building of 1718 having fallen victim to the demolition men in the 1960s the Friends converted a private house in Whitehead's Lane. Unwittingly they were renewing a link with their past. Whitehead's Lane, so Canon Jones tells us[22] was named after Manasseh Whitehead – and Manasseh Whitehead was a seventeenth century Bradford Quaker.

NOTES

1. The wimple helps to date the effigy. Fashionable between the late twelfth century and the mid-fourteenth century it was a length of white linen or silk draped over the front of the neck and brought up under the chin with the ends pinned to the hair over the ears.

2. The *Bishop's Bible* was a fresh English translation which, in 1571, Queen Elizabeth's Archbishop of Canterbury, Matthew Parker, ordered to be used in all churches.

3. See Country Life of 25 June 1964 - letter from Lawrence E Tanner, librarian Westminster Abbey – WANHS Library press cuttings book 22/259.
    Blomberg grew up at court with the king's other children and remained throughout life intimately connected with the royal family. In 1812 the Prince Regent presented him with the estate of Kirby Misperton, (near Pickering) Yorkshire.

    From Bradford on Avon Museum Society Newsletter No 7, October 1989:-
    Browsing through Bristol history books recently, your editor [Roger Clark], came across . . . a somewhat fantastic story put about to explain [Blomberg's] obscure origins. It seems that his father for some reason, in one version because of his secret marriage to a lady, had hidden him (and a sister in another version) by farming him out to foster parents. Unfortunately he was a soldier in the West Indies and was killed in action. That night his ghost appeared to a comrade and revealed the whereabouts of the boy and of papers which would prove his right to a fortune one day.
        Then, apparently Queen Charlotte heard the story of the miraculous revelation and had Frederic brought up at court.

4. James Budget (1765-1842). According to Robson's Commercial Directory for 1839 he was in business in the Old Market as grocer, cheesemonger, tallow chandler and agent for the Standard of England Life Office. The shop was at what is now number 32, facing Coppice Hill. where the Old Market Hall stood (see description later); the business subsequently became Budgett and Jones.

5. Fuller later became chief architect to the Canadian government, He designed the Parliament building in Ottawa in 1859 and also the cathedral and parish church of St Johns, Antigua.

6. Conveniently tabulated in *Wiltshire Meeting House Certificates 1689-1852,* published by the Wiltshire Record Society, editor J H Chandler.

7. *Baptists in Bradford on Avon* (1989).

8. This Francis Yerbury (1638-1720) was the grandfather of the Francis Yerbury who in 1766, as noted elsewhere, invented and patented cassimere.

9. Flexman was the distinguished theologian, scholar and historian. Renowned for his painstaking accuracy, in 1770 he was appointed by the government to compile a general index to the journals of the House of Commons.

10. Selina Hastings (1707-1791), Countess of Huntingdon, was an early Wesley supporter who later branched out to develop Calvinistic Methodism for the upper classes. John Wesley records in his Journal that on 5 October 1766 he administered the sacrament in her chapel in Bath. Among those present were the Lord Chancellor, Lord Chatham, Lord Bedford, the Bishop of Londonderry and other distinguished persons. Horace Walpole was there; a letter of 10 October 1766 to his friend John Chute comments on the occasion.

11. In his journal Wesley calls her 'Mrs. Ballard'. The 'Mrs. Bailward' he refers to later in the journal was Constant's daughter-in-law Anne (born Shewell) who married Constant's son John, in 1744. (see WRO 217/6, the marriage settlement document). Constant died later in the same year and was buried in the Quaker burial ground at Cumberwell. Constant's son John's name appears among the trustees of the Methodist chapel in 1767.

12. Not as paradoxical as might today appear. Water was unsafe and supply uncertain, beer comparatively wholesome and readily available. It was spirits, in particular gin, that were frowned upon; Hogarth's contemporary cartoons comparing the horrors of Gin Lane with the joys of prosperous Beer Street are *à propos*. Moderation was enjoined but total abstention was not practical policy till the next century.

13. The so-called 'chapel on the bridge'. It is a fairly typical Wiltshire blindhouse and dates from the seventeenth century. John Aubrey (1626-1697), probably writing from memory as he so often did, called it a chapel for mass. Aubrey was an amiable dilettante who dabbled in history and natural history and impoverished himself by a series of injudicious lawsuits. His descriptions tend to be inaccurate. As his is the only evidence we have of a chapel

on the town bridge there is reason to doubt if the building that he saw, which must be the one we see now, was ever other than what it was a century later when the hapless Hitchens was incarcerated in it. Did the weather-vane with its fish, the classic Christian symbol, confuse Aubrey? In the previous century the more reliable and painstaking John Leland described the bridge but said nothing of any chapel. If there ever was one surely he, a clergyman, would have mentioned it.

The little building has certainly had its vicissitudes. According to Canon Jones it was used at times as a toll-house, to take tolls on beasts going to the Saturday market. On the Ordnance Survey Map of 1924 it is shown as a magazine (*viz* ammunition store). About that time it was repaired and restored by public subscription and handed over by Sir Charles Hobhouse, the then owner, to the Wiltshire County Council.

14. Hitchens retired from preaching the following year (1758); he had been 'on the road' since 1745, and will have returned home to Cornwall. He was one of four brothers, all Methodist preachers, all much esteemed by John Wesley.

15. Anglican priest inclined towards Methodism who strove unsuccessfully to unite the two churches here and in North America, where he became a Methodist bishop. He was keen to promote the evangelisation of India. Early in 1813 he unsuccessfully applied to the Prime Minister, Lord Liverpool, for the appointment of Bishop in India. Undaunted, he set out for the sub-continent in December of that year but died on the voyage.

16. WRO 1699/18. In May 1660 Robert Storr was arrested while in meeting for worship at Cumberwell. He was brought before Justice Mitchell who refused to 'do anything concerning him as to imprisonment'. But he was nevertheless taken to Sarum and charged with being at an unlawful meeting. He was held in the town prison then brought before the magistrates who were told that he had been found at 'an unlawful assembly of rude and tumultuous people met together about three or four hundred to the disturbance of the peace of the nation... The magistrates 'did judge him to be a dangerous person'. He was imprisoned *sine die*.

17. Burials between 1700 and 1803, the last one that of Ann Eyles of Bradford, wife of James, aged 81. Now part of the car park.

18. Journal of Shomas Story, page 674. Quakers refused to swear an oath and after the Toleration Act of 1689 came into force were usually permitted to 'affirm' instead.

19. WRO 217/6. A trustee of the marriage settlement was leading Quaker Ezekiel Dickinsn of Monks, Corsham.

20. WRO 242 77/1

21. Minutes of Lavington Monthly Meeting of the Religious Society of Friends 13 September 1728 – WRO 1699/32.

22. WAM xx p.306: *A Walk through Bradford on Avon.*

5.
SCHOOLS

Right up to the early eighteenth century the notion that schooling was proper for other than the upper classes was alien to English thought. In the Middle Ages, and for some time after, such scraps of elementary education as were occasionally thrown to the poor came from the established church. As in the country at large so in Bradford. We have seen that Horton's Chantry included a school of sorts and we know from the records that in 1548 William Furbner the chantry priest was, single-handed, conducting it and that the vicar was expected to train children as choristers. Such instruction as was given will have had a bias to religious doctrine, in particular that of the established (then, of course, Roman Catholic) church. When the chantry was closed and its property seized the school continued for a while, still under Furbner, doctrine suitably modified no doubt. It was now supported by an annual grant from the Crown of ten pounds twelve shillings and sevenpence. But a few years later, in 1559, Furbner having died or given up (he would be about sixty-seven then) the authorities of the city of Salisbury seized the opportunity to get their hands on the money by persuading Queen Elizabeth that education was wasted on a town like Bradford and it would therefore be better paid to them. Thereafter, for about a century and a half, the town was without a school of any kind.

The Free Grammar School
In the reign of Queen Anne (1702-1714) the Church of England authorities, feeling threatened by the success of the schools being established by the dissenting sects, decided to set up free schools in competition to 'educate the children of the poor in reading, writing, moral discipline and the principles of the Church of England.' At the same time they tried, by the Schism Act of 1713, to suppress the dissenters' schools by making them unlawful. In this they failed. The dissenters refused to obey the law and

in 1718 succeeded in getting it repealed.

On 17 January 1712, the vicar of Bradford, John Rogers, set up a school for boys of the parish in the building we now know as the Saxon church. The project proved a success, so much so that three years later it was put on a sound footing by Ann Wright (formerly the Hon. Lady Ann Powlett) and her husband the Reverend Nathan Wright, the then lords of the manor. 'For the encouragement of learning and good manners within the parish of Bradford' they made over the building to William Methuen and eight others in trust to assure the school's continuance.

From then till the latter part of the nineteenth century the school continued to receive much local support. A clergyman, Edward Dike, gave £50 and another £50 was subscribed by local well-wishers. In about 1727 Francis Smith, a Bradford maltster, bequeathed the then substantial sum of £250 to be invested and the income made available for educating ten more poor Bradford children there. Edward Wadman was a supporter in the 1740s. In 1805 John Strawbridge of Bradford bequeathed £400; in 1850 John Bubb bequeathed £50 to educate four more poor Bradford boys; and in 1860 Hannah Smith left £50, the income from it to be used to augment the master's stipend.

What the school was like in the nineteenth century we know from the Charity Commission reports of 1834 and 1901 and from a printed sheet of rules and regulations. The master in 1834 was James Grist, who had been appointed in 1819. His salary was £40 a year and he lived on the premises rent and rates free. Instruction was in reading, writing and arithmetic only. There were fifty pupils. Of these, thirty-two were nominated by the trustees to receive free tuition but had to pay one shilling and eightpence a quarter for writing-books, pens and ink. The remainder paid fees, but all received the same instruction and received it on the same footing. Because places were much sought after, the maximum stay permitted was three years.

On weekdays school began at nine o'clock in the morning. In summer it ended at five o'clock in the afternoon and in winter at half past four. There was a break from half past twelve to two o'clock. Saturday afternoon was free. On Sunday pupils must present themselves at nine in the morning and half past five in the evening, and on that day and other days of divine service must attend church with the master, and sit in the gallery reserved for the school. Every boy must come clean in his person and dress; any failing in this respect were to be kept in after school or otherwise punished. Failure to attend church or school brought admonition, three admonitions meant expulsion. There were four weeks holiday every year, two in summer and two in winter. The summer holiday was in June, the winter one at Christmas. There was an examination once a year, on the Monday before the summer holiday began.

In 1834 the commissioners had described the building as being in a very dilapidated state. Little seems to have been done to remedy this, to judge by its condition when in 1874, as described elsewhere, the school trustees swapped it for Old Church House where the cross-wing at the north end of the building became the schoolroom, the rest of the building being rented off as cottages.

Old Church House. From 1874 to 1903 it was the free grammar school. It is now in part Trinity Church hall and in part Freemasons' Lodge.

By 1901 the school is beginning to sound a bit like Dotheboys Hall. There is still only one master, Frederick William Cowlishaw, who succeeded John Thornton Butt in 1875. Single-handed, in one 'long narrow high room', he teaches sixty boys of between the ages of seven and fourteen-plus. There is no playground. Basic teaching is still the three Rs, but between thirty and forty boys do either history or geography as well. In addition forty boys take drawing at an extra charge of seven shillings and sixpence a year. All do singing and 'drill' (physical exercises). It all seems very inadequate and yet Mr Cowlishaw is able to tell the commissioners that over the past three years twenty-five boys have entered the Civil Service (Post Office and Customs and Excise) by competitive examination and fifty-four have gone straight from school to become railway staff. We learn that Mr. Cowlishaw is a certificated teacher and a member of the College of Preceptors. Clearly he is no Wackford Squeers, however adverse his circumstances.

In 1899, largely as a result of misgivings which that distinguished resident Lord Edmond Fitzmaurice MP (1846-1935), (later Lord Fitzmaurice of Leigh), expressed about the school a public enquiry was held. The Hon. W N Bruce, an Assistant Commissioner under the Endowed Schools Acts, who conducted it, reported unfavourably. He found the school below standard, its finances mismanaged and its accounts badly kept. He commented that the sixty pupils were mainly sons of farmers and small tradesmen and were said to be of a different class from those using the public elementary schools. The Charity Commissioners accordingly recommended closure. They saw, they said, little likelihood of the establishment being run so as to offer any real educational advantage to the poor which was what the founders had intended. The trustees resisted, but in vain, and the school was closed in 1903.

National Schools and British Ones

By the early nineteenth century there was a growing awareness that England was falling behind the rest of Western Europe in the matter of education. In changing times it was felt that all children, however humble their background, should receive a measure of schooling. Progress was hampered by sectarian rivalry. For a long time the Church of England was dominant both at primary level and at the universities of Oxford and Cambridge from which, until 1871, non-Anglicans were barred. In 1807 progressives from both church and chapel, aiming to bridge sectarian differences in the interests of public education, formed the British and Foreign School Society. The policy was to set up schools, to be called British Schools, where the religious instruction would be non-denominational. In 1811 the Anglicans, no doubt feeling threatened, formed the National Society for the Education of the Poor according to the Principles of the Church of England to establish what they called National Schools. In these schools children would be taught not only the three Rs but also the catechism (sometimes summarised by the disrespectful as 'God bless the squire and his relations and keep us all in our proper stations'). They would also receive weekly visits by the vicar or his curate to ensure that religious instruction was sound.

In Bradford a British School was opened in the disused Quaker Meeting House. Quaker records show that the building was let, free of charge, as a school for poor children as early as 1806. In 1817 there was a formal agreement with Ezekiel Edmonds, Charles Cadby and William Taylor, all of Bradford on Avon, for the premises to be used as a British School for boys. The building stood in the area, now part of a car park, bounded by a dye-shop (now St Margaret's Hall), a house belonging to Charles Timbrell (now the Riverside Restaurant) and the house now called Westbury House. The school was popular; in 1830 average attendance was 140 to 200.

In 1836 the National Society and local Anglicans opened a rival establishment in Church Street which they called Trinity Church National School. This also was successful; in 1859 there were fifty to sixty boys and eighty to ninety girls. There was one master and one mistress. After 1880, when elementary education was made compulsory, numbers increased. In 1896 the school was enlarged to provide places for 157 boys, 168 girls and 204 infants. A new building was added on an adjacent site, with access from Newtown.

In 1847 a second National School called Christ Church School was opened at Mount Pleasant. When it came to the establishment of a Church of England school it was customary for a local landowner to donate the land on which it was to be built. Sir John Hobhouse, the Lord of the Manor, duly obliged and Captain S H Palairet paid for the building. With the continuing support of the local moneyed Christ Church School flourished. In 1878 an infants' school was erected on an adjoining site given by Miss Isabella Poynder (died 1880) of Leigh House. Miss Poynder had always taken a great interest in the school and she was accustomed to giving the pupils a treat from time to time. We know, for example, that in June 1867 she entertained 150 children to tea in her garden followed by singing, dancing to the violin, football and other delights. Then, children dismissed, the master and mistress (Caleb Bryant and his wife Mercy) and the pupil teachers stayed on for supper. We also know that in January 1869 she gave 167 scholars a hot dinner of roast beef, roast mutton, three kinds of vegetables, bread, plum pudding, mince pies and beer. Ten of her servants carved for and waited on the children. Miss Poynder would also give money prizes for outstanding work. For boys the prizes were for handwriting, arithmetic and mapping, for the girls needlework.

The British Schools (in 1860 one for girls had been started in Church Street - the 1871 census return shows that it was held in what had been until 1842 the Hobhouse Bank, now called Church House) enjoyed no such support. The boys' school went gradually downhill in increasingly decrepit surroundings. The final indignity came in 1880 when the building was declared by the Board of Education to be unfit for its purpose. The *Trowbridge Advertiser* of 25 September 1880 quoted the inspector's report '...ventilation most imperfect...smoke from neighbouring factory...effluvia from a rank and confined stable...position gloomy and depressing...no playground except the factory yard...' The press report added that leading nonconformists in the town were 'determined that unsectarian education shall not cease to be provided.' It so happened that about this time the nonconformists had built in Mason's Lane (on the site of a weaving workshop destroyed by fire in July 1869) a school for girls and infants. Known as the Undenominational School it will have succeeded the one in Church Street. With the closure of the building which had housed the boys' school the boys were transferred to this one.

From 1870, under the Elementary Education Act of that year, school boards could, if they wished, make by-laws compelling children aged five to twelve to attend school. Under the act of 1880 attendance was made compulsory for children up to the age of ten. They could then leave, if they had a certificate permitting them to do so, but could be made to stay to age thirteen if they had put in too few attendances

The twentieth century saw the demise of the old sectarian rivalries, though they died hard. The Undenominational School in Mason's Lane closed in the 1920s and its pupils were transferred to a newly built 'council' (*viz* non-sectarian) school in Trowbridge Road, now relocated and redesignated Fitzmaurice Primary School, with access from Frome Road. (The school building in Mason's Lane later became private houses, numbers 9, 10 and 10a) and since 1978 has been a centre of Buddhism in the Western Tharavadin tradition.

Christ Church Church of England School, now redesignated Christ Church Church of England Controlled Primary School, continues in new buildings on land adjacent to the old buildings, with access from Slades-brook.

Trinity School became, in the late 1940s, Trinity Secondary Modern School which in 1980, in accordance with national educational policy, merged with Fitzmaurice Grammar School to form St Laurence Voluntary Controlled Comprehensive School in new buildings in Ashley Road; now redundant, the 1836 building in Church Street was converted into flats and the 1896 one demolished to make way for sheltered housing called the Ropewalk.

Lord Fitzmaurice of Leigh in old age.

Fitzmaurice Grammar School

Lord Edmond Fitzmaurice, whose doubts about the value of the Free School in Old Church House eventually led to its closure in 1903, played a leading part in the establishment of the County Technical and Secondary School, later called, in his honour, the Fitzmaurice Grammar School. The first headmaster was John Crompton M.A. a mathematics exhibitioner of Jesus College, Oxford. The building was erected in Junction Road (architect J B Silcock) and opened in 1897. It continued in use until the Grammar School ceased to exist in its own right in 1980. It then came under threat of demolition for redevelopment; but local opinion in favour of its preservation prevailed and it became part of a sheltered housing scheme.

The new school had everything going for it. Where Mr Cowlishaw had been, with inadequate financial backing, coping single-handedly with sixty boys of various ages and abilities in one room (yet still getting acceptable results), the County School had spacious purpose-built classrooms, a vigorous and highly qualified headmaster, a headmistress (Miss Blake) and a staff of four full-time and three visiting teachers. Not surprisingly, from the time the rival establishment opened pupils had been drifting away from Mr Cowlishaw's school; the remnant will have transferred with the closure in 1903. In that year the County School had fifty-seven pupils of whom twenty were girls. Most of the pupils were of the white collar worker class, though one boy's father (as noted in the Board of Education school inspectors' report) was 'professional and independent'. Eight fathers were farmers and seven were artisans (skills unspecified). Fees were four pounds ten shilling a year.

John Crompton retired in 1926. In 1927 Board of Education inspectors recommended the introduction of what they called 'the House System ... to reproduce, so far as it is possible to do so in a day-school, the completeness of care and control of the individual pupil obtained in the great public schools.' So four 'houses' were created, two for boys and two for girls; one of them was named Crompton House, in honour of the first headmaster. Crompton had also been active in local affairs. Among other things he was a lieutenant in the Bradford Rifle Volunteers and a pillar of the Conservative Club.

Private Schools

A number of small private educational establishments have been run in Bradford at various locations at various times by private individuals. There was one for ten children in what is now St Mary's Chapel, Tory, according to the Rev. J Cox's *Magna Britannica* published between 1720 and 1731. In Pippett Street (now Market Street) in 1841 Miss Fanny Wilshire conducted an infants' school; she also took bookings for the coaches. We know of one at the Chantry; Charles Rawling's *Pictorial Guide* published in 1887 records that a Dr Knight had been master there and so had the Reverend Charles Thring. Thring, a curate at the parish church, had previously taught at Uppingham School, where his brother was headmaster. He lived on the premises with his wife Lydia and their family of five daughters and three sons. In 1893 there was a 'Young Gentlemen's Boarding School' at Avon Villas, Principal S S Lane Esq. B.A.; a 'High Class School for Girls' at Avon House, Principal Miss E F Watkins; and one 'Young Ladies' Seminary' at 6 St Margaret's Place, which was run by Mrs and Miss Vernon and another at Albert Terrace run by the Misses Harman. From 1895 to 1932 Miss Mabel Cockrom and her brother kept a 'Preparatory School for Young Ladies and Gentlemen under twelve years of age' at 28 St Margaret's Street.

Outside the town centre there was a private school at Pottick's House on the Bath road; *Kelly's Directory for Hampshire, Wiltshire and Dorset* for 1859 shows that Alfred H Mansell was then running a 'Gentlemen's Boarding School' there. Also on the Bath Road, Frankleigh House was being advertised in the Trowbridge Advertiser in 1879 as 'the Grammar School'. The building has continued in use as a private school, first as Kingswell Court, then as The Old Ride, then as Frankleigh House once again. The building has early seventeenth century origins with a major extension in 1848, see next chapter under 'Frankleigh House'.

There will also have been what were known as 'dame schools'. Daniel Batchelor (see later) seems to have attended one in about the early 1820s. It was kept by 'Ma'am' Dolls or Doles, in Coal Ash Walk, 'above Chantry'. Dame schools were at the lowest level, kept by a single untrained and probably ill-educated woman as a means of scraping a scanty living from the few pence paid by the poorest in the community. The best that can be said of them is that they were better than nothing and usually succeeded in teaching children to read.

6.
THE BUILDINGS

The toune self of Bradeford standith on the clining of a slaty rokke ...The toune is made al of stone ...   *John Leland*

I FINE HOUSES AND DISTINGUISHED OCCUPANTS

Three things in Bradford impressed Leland in 1540; the predominance of cloth manufacture; the wealthy families, enriched, like the Halls, by inherited land or, like the Hortons, by industrial enterprise; and the splendid stone houses.

THE HALL

The building that Leland called 'a pratie stone house at the este end of the towne' will most probably have been a typical hall of the Middle Ages. In its place, some half century after his visit, the present building was erected, probably by John Hall, doubtless larger and grander than its predecessor and certainly Bradford's most distinguished existing building.

But it was very nearly lost to the town. In 1805 it was sold to Thomas Divett, clothier, who erected a factory alongside called Kingston Mill. In about 1836 it was leased to Samuel Pitman, Trowbridge clothier,(father of Sir Isaac Pitman, inventor of the shorthand system called by his name). In 1848 the house, by that time in a state of near-dereliction, was restored by Stephen Moulton to what we see today. (The building contractor was James Long who also built the town hall – now the Church of St Thomas More – and the bank premises in Church Street formerly the North Wilts Bank, now Lloyd's). Re-roofed in 1981 by Dr Alex Moulton, the present owner, the house is safe for the foreseeable future.

The Hall was paid a nice compliment by the French in 1900; at the Paris exhibition they reproduced the south front for the English pavilion erected in honour of the visit of the Prince of Wales (later Edward VII).

The Hall, Bradford on Avon.

The Hall Family

The Halls were a prominent Bradford land-owning family from at least the mid-thirteenth century, the family name being written down then and later variously as 'Hall', 'at Halle', 'de Aula' and (by John Leland) 'de la Sale', all meaning the same thing, *viz* 'from the Hall' – the big house. John Hall founded the Hall's Almshouses in Frome Road and his arms may be seen on the building with the date AD 1700 and the inscription *Deo et pauperibus* (for God and the poor). John Hall left no male heir and on his death in 1711 the family name died out in Bradford.

Hall left all his property to Rachel Baynton, who, though she had been baptised (in April 1695) as the daughter of Thomas and Elizabeth Baynton, is said to have been his natural daughter. Through her marriage to William Pierrepont, son and heir of the Marquis of Dorchester, who later became the first Duke of Kingston, the Hall passed to their son Evelyn, second and last Duke of Kingston.

Elizabeth Chudleigh, Duchess of Kingston (1720-1788)

It was Evelyn whom Elizabeth Chudleigh, already married to Augustus Hervey, Earl of Bristol, bigamously married in 1769. Thereafter she resided with the Duke at The Hall. After the Duke's death in September 1773 she became the owner of that and the rest of his extensive property in other parts of the country. Her right to the property was questioned by the duke's heirs who saw to it that she was brought to trial charged with bigamy. Her five day trial in the House of Lords in April 1776 was, not surprisingly, a *cause célèbre*. Although she was found guilty she went unpunished and the property was held to be hers inalienably.

She died suddenly in Paris on 26 August 1788. In a mere matter of weeks a book called *Authentic details and particulars relative to the late Duchess of Kingston* (author unnamed) appeared in print with a venomous account of the lady's shortcomings, real or invented. So promptly did it appear that it seems likely that the late Duke of Kingston's bitterly disappointed heirs had put it together during her lifetime and, wary of the law of libel, waited for the moment of death to publish.

I found a copy of the book in St Deiniol's Library, Hawarden. Facing the title page is an engraving of a full length portrait of the duchess by Thomas Gainsborough. This is stated to be as she appeared dressed as Iphigenia, at a ball given by the Venetian Ambassador at Somerset House in 1744. Presumably the duchess had had the painting done and there is nothing unusual about the costume; but according to the book she was, on that occasion 'everything but naked' and like her first parents in the Garden of Eden, 'unashamed'.

The book is full of derogatory, sometimes scandalous, anecdotes. She is stated to have kept pistols by the side of her bed and to have given instructions to her servants never to enter her room unless the bell rang, in case, taken by surprise, she should shoot them. When at her trial the verdict of guilty was pronounced she is said to have whispered to her counsel Mr Glover 'There are blunderbusses and pistols at Kingston House. Go there directly and turn all the servants out of doors and keep possession of the house for me by force.'

It is alleged that she changed her friends 'like garments' and that the only permanent attachments she had were with those she seldom saw. In St. Peterburg, where she went to live, her eccentric behaviour is said to have been a byword. Feeling the call of nature when out one day she went into a cabinet-maker's shop, sent the owner on a 'frivolous commission' and while he was absent calmly relieved herself in a piece of his furniture 'commodious for the purpose'. Her friend the Czarina Catherine (Catherine the Great) is said to have found the story highly amusing.

The duchess's will made on 7 October 1756 is given in full in the book. The last codicil to it was made 21 August 1787. It was proved in September 1788. She died possessed of very great wealth in the form of lands in England and abroad. She owned a number of serfs and the will as reproduced here refers to four musical slaves and their wives who were to have their liberty for six years after her death and after that to remain in bondage for the rest of their lives.

In the words of the writer of the *Authentic Details and Particulars*: 'The duchess had through life distinguished herself as a most eccentric character. Her turn of mind was original and many of her actions were without a parallel...if others invited admiration by partial display of their charms at a masquerade she at once threw off the veil ...The duchess had an apparent attachment for the Bishop of Wilna. She also when in Rome discovered something more than friendship for the Patriarch of Jerusalem'. She was also said to have included Pope Clement XIV among her men friends.

Elizabeth Chudleigh's way of life and indifference to public opinion seem to have been outstanding even for the age in which she lived. But I wonder what the rebutting evidence might have been if the allegations had been made in her lifetime. What is detailed in the book is almost certainly not out of the writer's own experience but a retailing of gossip and tittle-tattle. Whether she was fairly described we shall never know now, but she was, unquestionably, a remarkable character.[1]

The Moulton Family

Stephen Moulton (1794-1880) was born in Whorlton, County Durham. In 1827 he married Elizabeth Riche and subsequently settled in New York. In 1847 they returned to England to settle in Bradford on Avon, where, as we have seen, Stephen set up as a manufacturer of rubber. Three sons, Alexander (died 1885), Horatio (1837-1893) and John (1839-1925) in due course joined their father in the firm. Alexander succeeded him and was head of the firm for the five years till his death. In 1891 the brothers Horatio and John joined forces with their father's old friend George Spencer to form George Spencer, Moulton and Co. Horatio became chairman and on his death was succeeded by John.

The family have a distinguished record of public service and conservation in the town. John served with distinction on District and County Councils and was High Sheriff for the county in 1917. With Lord Edmond Fitzmaurice he was a major donor of the public baths and pleasure ground on the south bank of the river, now, alas, become a mere public car park; the iron railings on the river side bearing the initial letters JM in the form of a monogram are all that remain of a once pleasant haven.

The last bearer of the family name still living in the town is Dr Alex Moulton, great-grandson of Stephen. Dr Moulton, who describes himself as 'an innovating engineer' is best known as the inventor of the Moulton bicycle; but he is distinguished also as the inventor of *Flexitor*, a type of trailer suspension. Rubber suspension designed by him was used in the British Leyland Mini and his Hydrolastic suspension was used for the Austin/Morris 1100/1300 range. Later on his Hydragas suspension (which replaced rubber suspensions by gas-sprung ones) were adopted by British Leyland for the Austin Metro and Austin Ambassador. Hydragas received the Queen's Award to Industry in 1967.

ABBEY HOUSE, CHURCH STREET, BRADFORD ON AVON, AND WESTWOOD MANOR, WESTWOOD.

Almost nothing remains of the 'very fair house of the building of one Horton' which John Leland saw and noted. The early eighteenth century Abbey House is a partial rebuilding of it, with a remnant of the original at the back. The building now called Trinity Church Hall which Thomas Horton built has, however, survived and externally at least is very much as Leland will have seen it.

Abbey House was once the home of clothier Ezekiel Edmonds, who later lived at Berryfield House.

Besides the house which Leland saw, Thomas Horton also owned Westwood Manor House (about 1½ miles south-west of Bradford) from about 1513. The original building, erected before 1400, had been a modest farmhouse on land held under the Priory of Winchester. In 1480 Thomas Culverhouse, owner then, enlarged it substantially. Thomas Horton enlarged it still more. Clearly to be included in his contribution is the present dining-room. On the left and right spandrels of the fireplace are carved respectively the initials T and H. In the bedroom above the dining-room the oriel window contains a roundel of stained glass with a rebus formed by the three letters HOR over a barrel or tun. (This is a copy of the original which was removed and placed in the church just before 1900).

Westwood Manor is now National Trust property.

The Horton Family

The Hortons claimed descent from Roger de Horton, Justice of Cheshire in 1428. They are said to have been drawn to the West of England by the prospect of riches from the clothing industry. If so they were not disappointed; by the early sixteenth century they owned land at Trowbridge, North Bradley, Southwick, Westbury, Rode, Frome, Wolverton, Bradford, Westwood, Iford, Farleigh, Hinton, Chippenham, Foxham, Sevington, Tilshead, Cheverill, Cricklade, Corsley, Tellisford and Freshford. Later on they were to do well out of Henry VIII's dissolution of the monasteries.[2] Thomas Horton (died 1530), the Bradford benefactor, included in his property Westwood Manor and Iford Manor and built the substantial house in Bradford in which he lived. Thomas was a great churchman. His Bradford home was as near to the parish church as he could get it: '... at the north est part by the chirch' as John Leland observed. He built the church hall. And to the parish church he added, in what is now the north aisle, a chantry chapel; the brass recording this, formerly set in the chapel floor, is now on the east wall of the north aisle. At Westwood either he or his nephew Thomas built the church tower; the initials TH are above the entrance. In his will he left property to Hinton Charterhouse Priory.

Thomas Horton died childless and his property went to his nephew of the same name. This Thomas seems to have moved out of Bradford, probably to Iford; when Leland visited the town (in the early 1540s) he noted that 'one Lucas, a clothier, now dwelleth in Horton's house.' (Thomas's wife Mary's maiden name had been Lucas so the property was evidently still in the family). Nephew Thomas died in 1549 and in his will he left, among other estate, 'all the lands ... acquired from King Henry VIII'. He had evidently been on very good terms with that monarch – as noted earlier, when his uncle's chantry was dissolved he had succeeded in acquiring some of the chantry endowment. Thomas's daughter Alice married into the Yerbury family, as to whom see later.

PRIORY HOUSE, Market Street

At the time of Leland's visit in 1540 another fine house in the town was the one belonging to Thomas Rogers, Serjeant-at-Law. Priory House in Market Street is lineally descended from the house probably built by him in about 1460. Hardly anything remains of the original edifice except perhaps the wall on to Market Street which, as can readily be seen, was once the outside wall of part of a building.

From 1657 the house was owned by the Methuen family. John Methuen (died 1706) who, as described elsewhere, negotiated, as ambassador to Portugal, the important Methuen Treaty of 1703, will have been born there.

The Methuen family were owners until 1763 when they sold to the Tugwell family. In 1811 Mawbey Tugwell (died 1815) sold the property to fellow-clothier John Saunders, who added the kitchen wing – which is all that remains today of the building he knew.

John was succeeded by his son Thomas Hosier Saunders, partner in the clothing firm of Saunders, Fanner and Saunders[3] who in turn was succeeded by his son Thomas Bush Saunders, who departed from family tradition and became a barrister. Up to that time the property had been known as Methuen's but Thomas Bush Saunders seems to have decided to call it The Priory even before he leased it to a detachment of the Sisters of the Holy Trinity for a few years in the 1850s. (In the 1871 census return it is called the *Old* Priory.)

When Thomas Bush Saunders died in 1894 the property went to his daughter Mrs Collett. Within the next half century it changed hands twice more, in 1930 and 1937. In 1937 it had been unoccupied and on the market for some time. The estate of some 14½ acres was therefore broken up into lots and sold for development and in the following year almost all the ancient house was pulled down. The fifteenth century porch was salvaged by the Methuen family and moved to Corsham Court.

The splendid tulip tree which John Saunders planted remains to this day. (When Canon Jones's history was revised by John Beddoe in 1907 a second one was extant).

The stone barn which formed part of the property until 1937 belongs now to the Bradford on Avon Preservation Trust.

The site itself may well be one of great antiquity. A modest exploratory dig in 1978 by Mrs Pamela Slocombe revealed, besides medieval and

*Above: Priory House, late Georgian extension of the medieval mansion
Below: Clothing magnate Humphrey Tugwell (1704-75) and his wife Elizabeth
(1711-1801) 'constant and liberal benefactress of the poor' lived in the old house.
(Thomas Gainsborough's portraits are reproduced here by kind permission of Sir
Mervyn Medlycott, Bt, their descendant, and courtesy of The Paul Mellon Centre
for Studies in British Art).*

possibly Saxon sherds, Roman artefacts consisting of a piece of combed box tile and a sherd of grey hard fabric, with single line incised decoration. Roman coins were found in the garden in 1818.

Thomas Rogers (fl.1460)

Thomas Rogers was a serjeant-at-law, a legal bigwig appointed personally by the sovereign. Together with the extensive land-ownership at Bradford, Cumberwell and Holt, Thomas will have been a man of considerable consequence nationally as well as locally.[4] Thomas's grandson Sir Edward Rogers (died 1582) held the even more important office of Comptroller of the Household to Queen Elizabeth.

John Methuen (c 1650-1706)

John Methuen was Member of Parliament for Devizes from 1690 to 1705 and was envoy to Portugal in 1691 and 1702 and ambassador in 1703, the year in which he negotiated the famous Methuen Treaty. He was Chancellor of Ireland for seven years.

According to Canon Jones he was the statesman alluded to in John Home's famous lines:-

> *Firm and erect the Caledonian stood*
> *Old was his mutton and his claret good*
> *Let him drink port, the English statesman cried*
> *He drank the poison, and his spirit died.*

Paul Methuen (1672-1757)

John Methuen's son Paul succeeded his father as ambassador to Portugal in 1706 and remained in post till 1708. He then became Member of Parliament for Devizes. He held office in government on and off until 1730. He died unmarried and was buried near his father in Westminster Abbey. He left £250,000 of which £50,000 was in gold coins, found in sealed bags in the house. Horace Walpole called him 'a dull, formal, romantic braggadochio'. But John Gay wrote of him:

> *Methuen of sincerest mind*
> *As Arthur grave, as soft as womankind.*

The town of Methuen, Massachusetts, was named after him.

Thomas Bush Saunders (1808-94)

Thomas Bush Saunders is remembered as the restorer of the chapel of St. Mary, Tory (John Leland's 'chapelle on the highest place of the towne' which, when he bought it in 1889, was little more than a ruin. Saunders was a barrister of Lincoln's Inn and Queen's Counsel but by 1871 was no longer in practice. In retirement he was a senior magistrate and chairman of the Bradford on Avon District Council.

CHANTRY HOUSE, Church Street

When Thomas Horton founded his chantry in 1524 in what is now the north aisle of the parish church he provided also the 'mantyon house of the chantry'. Much enlarged it has come down to us, its name essentially intact after a varied career as private house, clothier's business premises and private school. It is now divided into two private houses called respectively Chantry House and Little Chantry.

Little Chantry is what we see as we walk past the parish church on the left. Chantry House, to the rear, contains the original building, a feature of which is a built-in stone tank constantly replenished with fresh water by a rivulet flowing through; this will have been a kind of larder of fresh fish for the table, possibly also a place for breeding fish. Over this is a small room said to have been a priest's room or place of concealment.

Chantry House

In 1548 King Edward VI dissolved the chantry and sold the house to Thomas Horton, a nephew of the founder of it (see above). It remained a private house up to 1794 when it was leased to John Yerbury, clothier, as his home and business premises. Yerbury added a factory building and purchased adjoining land giving access to the river, which he used thereafter to transport goods to and from Avoncliff where his brother-in-law John Moggridge had recently built a factory and workers' accommodation. (This, in the straitened times of the next century, became the overfull workhouse; later still it became successively a wartime military hospital, a hotel and, finally, residential accommodation.)

Chantry House stayed domestic/industrial for the next half century. It was used as such successively by Ebenezer Brown (from 1807 to 1810) and Samuel Mundy and Co. (up to about 1842), when Samuel Mundy, like so many other Bradford clothiers at that time, went out of business. The factory was pulled down and the house was used for some years as a small private school. From 1891 it was the home of John Beddoe, a private house once again.

Samuel Cam and the Hobhouse Family

Samuel Cam (died 1792) lived at Chantry House from 1741, having bought it when the previous owner, Edward Thresher, died. From humble origins Cam had grown rich in the clothing trade.

A memorial tablet in Holy Trinity church, Bradford on Avon, erected in 1794 by Benjamin Hobhouse states that Samuel Cam, Justice of the Peace, died 7 November 1792, that his first wife was Elizabeth and that she bore him ten children, one of whom, Maria Teresa, married Isaac Hillier. Samuel's second wife was Mary.

Mary bore three daughters, one of whom, Charlotte, married Benjamin Hobhouse, barrister, in 1785. Charlotte and Benjamin had three sons and one daughter.

Charlotte and her father were Presbyterians with, like so many other members of the congregation at the Grove Chapel (of which Samuel was a generous benefactor), a marked leaning to Unitarianism. Charlotte, as soon as her firstborn little son John Cam Hobhouse was old enough, sent him to the school at Bristol conducted by eminent Unitarian preacher and schoolmaster John Prior Estlin.

Charlotte died in 1791 and her father died the following year, whereupon Benjamin Hobhouse became owner and, for a short while, occupier. He kept up his Bradford connexions but his ambitions were in national politics. These ambitions were realised; in due course he became Chief Secretary of the Board of Control for India. He was created baronet in 1812.

John Cam Hobhouse (1786-1869) also made politics his career, but not until he was well into his thirties. Perhaps a strict Puritan upbringing plus intimate friendship with the raffish Lord Byron from their time together at Cambridge University was the explosive mixture which governed his anti-establishment stance for many years and eventually landed him in gaol for a brief spell; for his openly expressed approval of Napoleon Bonaparte and his attacks on the French monarchy and British government policy he was sent to Newgate on 14 December 1819 for alleged breach of parliamentary privilege. Luckily for him, the old parliament was dissolved at the end of February 1820, whereupon he was released and at the ensuing election the tables were turned and he became a member of the new one. Thereafter he pursued an extremely successful career, becoming in turn Secretary for War, Chief Secretary for Ireland and President of the Board of Control. In 1851 he was created Baron Broughton of Broughton Gifford.

Benjamin's second son, Benjamin, was killed at Waterloo.

Henry William Hobhouse (1791-1868) was Member of Parliament for Hereford. He was also a partner, with his father and Charles Phillott and Charles Lowder, in the local private banking firm of Hobhouse, Phillott and Lowder, which had branches in Bath and Church Street, Bradford on Avon. He also had links with India, having been employed there for a time by the East India Company.

The present baronet and Lord of the Manor of Bradford, Sir Charles John Spinney Hobhouse, of Monkton Farleigh Manor, succeeded his father in January 1991.

John Beddoe (1826-1911)

John Beddoe was born at Bewdley in Worcestershire. He was in medical practice in Bristol from 1857 to 1890 with a short break when he served as an army doctor in Turkey during the war in the Crimea. He retired to Bradford in 1891. In 1907 he re-published 'with notes and continuation' Canon Jones's classic history of the town, first published in the Wilts

Archaeological Magazine in 1859, together with an article on the Hall by Canon Jackson first published in the same magazine in 1854.

Beddoe was a keen anthropologist, particularly interested in head shapes and colour of eyes and hair, on which subjects he wrote a number of articles in learned publications. He was a Fellow of the Royal Society and an active member of the Anthropological Institute and of the Anthropological Society of London, on both of which bodies he served as president.

CHURCH HOUSE, Church Street

This handsome Georgian house was from 1821 to 1842 the banking premises of Hobhouse, Phillott and Lowder. The owner was then Sir Benjamin Hobhouse; the bankers were Sir Benjamin himself, his second son Henry William, Charles Phillott and Charles Lowder. When the bank failed in 1841 the property was bought by Thomas Wheeler who leased the ground floor to the North Wilts Bank who later moved into new premises adjoining, now Lloyd's Bank. From 1860 the building was for a number of years the British School for Girls.

Church House, one-time premises of Hobhouse, Phillot and Lowder.

WESTBURY HOUSE, St Margaret's Street

Westbury House, formerly Bethell House, was built in the early eighteenth century.

In 1791 it was the scene of an ugly riot (described elsewhere) by unemployed cloth-workers against the then owner, Phelps, a clothier who had introduced machinery into his factory. Not long after this Dr Bethell, a physician, became the owner. He was the father of Richard Bethell, first Lord Westbury. Subsequent owners were George Spencer, of Spencer, Moulton and Co, and Charles Adye, County Architect. From 1911 to 1973 the house was the offices of the Bradford Urban District Council. It has since been converted into flats.

Richard Luttrell Pilkington Bethell, 1st Lord Westbury (1800-73) was born in Westbury House. He was educated first at Corsham (presumably the Dame Margaret Hungerford School) then at Bristol. At the age of fourteen he entered Wadham College, Oxford, He took his degree at the age of eighteen and was made a fellow of his college.

In 1823 he became a barrister and rapidly built up a first-class practice. In 1851 he became Liberal Member of Parliament for Aylesbury and in the following year was knighted and made Solicitor General in the government of Lord Aberdeen. Later he became Attorney General ,and in 1861, Lord Chancellor, and was elevated to the peerage as Lord Westbury of Westbury.

In 1865 he fell from grace a little following a scandal in connexion with Leeds Bankruptcy Court. Though he was not personally involved, a motion of censure in the House of Commons declared him negligent in not having detected what was going on. In consequence he had to resign, though, his character not in question, he continued to sit as one of the Lords of Appeal.

DRUCE'S HILL HOUSE, Church Street

This attractive house was described, in a survey of 1738-40 (in the Dean and Chapter's records in the Bristol Record Office), as 'new-built'. It then belonged to Anthony Druce, who came of a long line of Druces whose name appears, from the mid-sixteenth century on, in parish church registers, lists of churchwardens and in various property transactions. (Canon Jones, incidentally, writes of an Anthony and a William Druce as Quakers but their names do not appear as such in any of the Quaker

Westbury House

Druce's Hill House

records in the County Record Office.)

Anthony Druce was not owner for long. The house passed out of his possession when he became bankrupt in about 1740 and it is pretty certain that he, at least, was not a Quaker. If he had been, his bankruptcy would normally have been recorded and deplored in the Quaker minute book of the day – and it is not. (Among eighteenth century Quakers failure in business was tantamount to sin; such a rare event was always closely investigated and evidence of negligence or culpability could result in expulsion from membership). But later in the century the house came into the possession of the Bailward family, who, as we have seen, *were* Quakers and this may be what the Canon had in mind. The house remained in the Bailwards' ownership until well into the last century.

KINGSTON PLACE, formerly The Vicarage

John Leland noted the existence of a vicarage 'at the west ende of the chirch' and the present building, largely Victorian, doubtless occupies the same site and includes some, at least, of the original building. It was the home of the celebrated Canon W H R Jones when he was vicar from 1851 till his death in 1885.

Canon William Henry Rich Jones (1817-85)

Canon Jones is remembered for his discovery of the Saxon church, as described earlier, for his work on the Domesday Book and for his classic history of the town, first published in the form of articles in the Wiltshire Archaeological Magazine by the Wiltshire Archaeological and Natural History Society, of which he was vice president.

Jones was born at Blackfriars and educated at King's College, London, and Magdalen Hall (now Hertford College) Oxford, where he won the prize for Sanskrit. Before his appointment to Bradford in 1851 he had been Rector of the church of St Martin-in-the-Fields and of St James's, Shoreditch. He died suddenly at the vicarage on 28 October 1885.

It was the historically-minded Canon Jones who persuaded the authorities to re-name our town from Great Bradford, as it was called when he first came, to the name it bore in AD 652, Bradford on Avon.

Orpin's House

ORPIN'S HOUSE and Edward Orpin (1692-1781)

This attractive small house in Church Street probably dates back to the late seventeenth century. An unusual feature is the pair of square 'bottle glass' windows set in the wall, the aim being, it is said, to reduce liability to window tax. Edward Orpin lived here for many years with his first wife Anna and, after her death, with his second wife, widow Sarah Taplin, born Ferrett, sister of John Ferrett the Bradford on Avon benefactor. After Sarah's death Orpin married, in 1749, widow Ruth Pinnell.

Orpin was a local official whose name and signature appear frequently in the vestry records. He came of a family of small Bradford tradesmen engaged in brewing, baking and inn-keeping. He himself began life as a cooper. Orpin was well-educated by the standards of the day, though we do not know of a school in Bradford on Avon until 1712, when Orpin would have been twenty and well over school age. His official duties were varied. He attended meetings of the vestry, transcribed registers, was Coroner of the Market[7] and collected unpaid tithes; in the latter connexion we find him named in Quaker records[8] as having seized in 1729 four lambs from Joseph Hull 'on account of John Rogers, Vicar. Not exceeding demand'. (Hull had refused, as a Quaker, to pay dues to the Anglican church authorities.)

Although Charles Rawling states, in his 1887 *Pictorial Guide*, that when Gainsborough and his friend the actor Garrick lived in Bath they used to visit Orpin in Bradford on Avon, the following extract from an article by W J Loftie in *The Architectural Review* of February 1905 suggests otherwise; Loftie wrote:

> The history of Edward Orpin, who died in his own house at Bradford in 1781 is variously related in the local guide-books, most of them making him the friend of the great artist who was living and painting at number 24 in the Circus at Bath between 1760 and 1774...The truth for once seems to lie with a local tradition, now apparently locally forgotten, but well remembered in 1866, when Mr Wiltshire, the descendant and successor of Gainsborough's friend, died at his house, Shockerwick, in Somersetshire, which lies a short distance east of Bathford on the Corsham Road...It became the custom, certainly in summer, that the artist should spend the 'week's end' with his friend the carrier, Mr Wiltshire, who always refused payment for conveying Gainsborough's pictures to London. On Sunday evenings the parish clerk used to come over the intervening hills in order to read the Bible to the Shockerwick household, and this was probably Gainsbor-

Canon Jones

ough's sole acquaintance with Orpin, who sat perhaps unwittingly to be immortalised.

I well remember the seven fine pictures, five of which, and among them the portrait of Orpin, hung over the bookcase in the library. Early the following year they were removed to London and sold at Christie's. I was told in the house that they had hung as they were during the auction of the furniture from the time they were painted. The last Mr Wiltshire had lived for many years in great retirement, and nothing had been removed. There were portraits of Foote and Quin the actors, and two of local scenes, gipsies and boys with dogs, besides the two grand landscapes in the adjoining room, *The Harvest Wagon*, in which there was a portrait of Miss Wiltshire as well as of the artist's daughters, and the *Cattle and Figures* which was also a view in Shockerwick Park... *The Parish Clerk* was bought for the National Gallery for £325 ten shillings...

It was long thought, as Loftie and the National Gallery did, that the picture *The Parish Clerk*, now in the possession of the Tate Gallery, was a portrait of Edward Orpin by Thomas Gainsborough. The Tate Gallery, however, now state that the work is not Gainsborough's, and attribute it to Nathaniel Hone (1718-1784). So we have a mystery awaiting solution. Who did paint the picture and is it of Orpin? The Tate Gallery say that there is a portrait of what appears to be the same person in the J.G. Johnson Collection at the Philadelphia Museum of Art.

BRADFORD ON AVON TOWN CLUB, 29 Market Street

This was the site of the Maidenhead Inn, malthouse and brewhouse from some time before 1611. In 1755 Methodist innkeeper Richard Pearce bought the property, renovated the inn, (the front elevation dates from then) and demolished the malthouse to make way for a Methodist chapel. The chapel continued in use until the opening of a larger one on Coppice Hill in 1818. In the 1840s the building was taken over by Joseph Rawling for his printing business and Joseph's son Charles continued there from his father's death in 1866 to his own in 1903.

In 1903 John Moulton bought the property on behalf of the Conservative Club, refurbished it and in the following year leased it to them as their new premises. On John Moulton's death in 1925 the property was bought by a newly-formed non-political social club, the present Bradford on Avon Club.

OLD BANK HOUSE, Bridge Street

The house probably dates back to the fifteenth century. In the 18th century it was a pub called the Red Lyon, belonging to the Duke of Kingston who at first leased then sold it and the adjoining bullpit to John Moggridge, clothier. Moggridge erected a factory on what had been the bullpit and probably lived in the house. In 1812 it seems to have come into the ownership of a member of the Yerbury family. (John Moggridge was brother-in-law of the John Yerbury of Chantry House.)

From about 1820 Joseph Rawling ran a printing press and stationery business there. In 1875 we find John James Rawling acting as agent there for the Wilts and Dorset Banking Co Ltd and by 1885 the building housed a fully-fledged branch of that bank. By 1915 the bank was no longer listed in local directories.

Joseph Rawling (1792-1866)

Rawling was born and grew up in Exeter. As a boy he was converted to Methodism and became a lay preacher at the age of 18. He worked as a printer, first in Bristol, where in 1815 he married, then in Bath.

Shortly after his grandfather's death in 1816 he came to Bradford and set up on his own as a printer and bookseller, at first with small success. Business improved after 1820 following the move to Church Street. Trade directories show that he was trading as printer, bookseller, stationer, account book manufacturer and agent for the Sun, Fire and Eagle Life Office 'and all the London newspapers'. The 1841 tithe map shows that in that year he was still in business at the Church Street premises and that he was also owner of what is now 6 Pippet Buildings. Shortly afterwards he moved to 29 Market Street.

Joseph Rawling, besides being the town's printer, became, from 1852, the postmaster. His post office was next door (now number 28).

The Rawling family business printed, published and sold a wide range of good quality material from handbills to bound books. In 1865 Joseph Rawling wrote an autobiography which he printed, published and sold at the Pippet Street premises.

There is a stained glass window to his memory in the parish church.

Old Bank House in Church Street was Joseph Rawling's printing press and stationer's shop from 1820.

5, ST MARGARET'S STREET (THE LIBERAL CLUB)

This late seventeenth or early eighteenth century grade II listed building was the home of Joseph Chaning Pearce (1806-47). Pearce, a surgeon by profession, practised in Church Street in partnership with his father, James Chaning Pearce (1775-1850). Father and son were both keen collectors of fossils but from the age of five it was Joseph's chief interest in life; as an infant he would insist on picking up fossils from the wayside, much to his nurse's concern. The coming of the railways with their deep cuttings provided for him a happy hunting ground and he retired from practice in 1845 so as better to concentrate on his hobby. He was especially interested in marine carnivorous reptiles. The Pearces' large collection was kept in the St Margaret's Street house till father and son both moved to Bath in 1845. Their collection became famous throughout Europe.

Joseph Chaning, Pearce's son, also named Joseph Chaning Pearce and also a medical practitioner, sold the collection to the Bristol Museum.

WOOLLEY HILL HOUSE, 18 Woolley Hill (also called Woolley Hill Lodge)

This is a Grade II listed building, re-fronted in 1804. At the beginning of the present century the house was the home of Frank Applegate, owner of Greenland Mill and the last clothier to operate in Bradford on Avon. It was in the kitchen of Woolley Hill House that stonemason Bertram Niblett was startled to find, hidden by a flagstone precariously resting over it, a cavernous well deeper than the house was high.[9]

To Woolley Hill House Bradford on Avon is indebted for a footnote in the history of French literature. From an article in 1975 by Eileen Holt and L J Austin in *French Studies* (a quarterly periodical published by the Taylor Institution of St Giles, Oxford) we learn that it was here in 1871 that Stéphane Mallarmé (1842-78) penned a poem *Dans le Jardin*, which begins

La jeune dame qui marche sur la pelouse...

The garden was that of Woolley Hill House, which in those days stood in six acres, and the young lady was Ellen (1840-1925), wife of fellow-poet William Charles Bonaparte-Wyse (1826-92), the then owner. Mallarmé was their house-guest for a few days. Bonaparte-Wyse, Ango-Irish on his father's side and French on his mother's – she was a niece of Napoleon Bonaparte – had met Mallarmé when travelling in Provence in the 1860s, about the time that Bonaparte-Wyse had published a collection of poems in Provençal. Bonaparte-Wyse, who, as touched upon in the poem, was a sick man while living here, returned to his native Ireland in 1872.

Mallarmé was active in the symbolist movement in poetry, which began in France between 1880 and 1895 and later spread elsewhere.

BELCOMBE COURT, WELLCLOSE HOUSE and the Yerburys

A characteristic of the seventeenth, eighteenth and nineteenth centuries was the growing concentration of wealth in the hands in certain families, very often through intermarriage between members of the same nonconformist religious persuasion. Some of the fine houses that have come down to us were built or extended by such families, among whom we can include the Presbyterian Yerburys.

Belcombe Court stands on Belcombe Road some three quarters of a

Above: Belcombe Court, home of the Yerbury family for nearly two centuries. Below: Wellclose House.

mile to the west of the town centre. John Yerbury (1678-1728) built on the site, which he acquired in 1722, a clothier's house and factory combined, a fairly typical arrangement in those days. He called it Bellcombe Brook House. In 1734 John's son Francis (1706-1778) engaged John Wood the Elder to re-style the building. Wood added two wings in classic style redolent of his work in Bath, where he designed Queen's Square and the Circus. The barn on the east side of the house, once thought to be of medieval origin, is now believed to have been constructed in the late eighteenth century.

The house remained the property of the Yerbury family until 1903 when John William Yerbury sold it to one Samuel Francis.

A short distance from Belcombe Court is Wellclose House. Francis's brother Joseph John was living there at the time that Francis was gentrifying the former and it seems likely that John Wood was engaged to re-front the latter. The work was on the pretentious side for a building which was in reality a nice old farmhouse.

The Yerburys were prosperous Bradford clothiers from at least the early seventeenth century. They were also active Presbyterians. Official records show that Francis Yerbury (1638-1720) had his house and a barn (called Kelson's Barn) registered in 1692 as Presbyterian places of worship and that in 1698 Francis Yerbury the Elder and Francis Yerbury the Younger (presumably father and son), with others, were purchasers from Anthony Methuen of land on which to build the Grove Chapel (see above)). Joseph John, the one who lived at Wellclose House and re-fronted it, was said by Canon Jones to have been a Quaker but the writer has been unable to confirm this from Quaker records.

Francis (1706-1778), son of the builder of Belcombe Court, trained in London as a barrister but returned to the Bradford clothing business bringing to it a weaving method which he is said to have learned from the silk weavers of Spitalfields. He patented this in 1766 as 'a new method of making thin superfine cloth for the summer season at home, and warmer climates abroad, and yet notwithstanding the thinness of the texture, it is more durable than cloth of a greater substance made in the common way'. The material came to be known as cassimere (sometimes called kerseymere).

In 1787 Belcombe was the scene of what might have developed into a serious riot. Some 1500 rebellious weavers from Trowbridge marched on Bradford. On arriving at Belcombe Brook they found that John William

Yerbury (who had succeeded his father Francis at Belcombe) had mounted two small cannon in the windows to intimidate them. Whether because of the cannon or of John William's eloquence or because Bradford weavers failed to support them, they turned back, their purpose, whatever it was, unaccomplished.

John William Yerbury was one of the sponsors when the Grove Meeting House was somewhat belatedly registered as a place of worship in 1793.

BERRYFIELD HOUSE (sometimes called Bearfield House)

The house, which in 1979 became Bradford on Avon hospital, and for some years before that had been the maternity hospital, was built in the early nineteenth century.

In mid-century it was the home of clothier Ezekiel Edmonds[9], Member of Parliament (Liberal), vigorous opponent of the Corn Laws, Deputy Lieutenant for the County, magistrate, and founder member of the Bradford on Avon corps of the Wiltshire Rifle Volunteers.

Berryfield House, now Bradford on Avon Hospital.

Later in the century Gerald Augustus Robert Fitzgerald (born 1844) lived there. He was a barrister, son of A O Fitzgerald, Archdeacon of Wells. After that it became the home of Brigadier-General Palmer, a Territorial Army officer who served in the First World War and commanded successively the Royal Wiltshire Yeomanry and the 10th Mounted Brigade. From 1918 to 1922 Brigadier Palmer was Member of Parliament for the Westbury constituency. He died at Bexley, Kent, in 1932.

WOOLLEY GRANGE (formerly WOOLLEY HOUSE), now WOOLLEY GRANGE HOTEL.

This house dates back to the late 1600s. It was owned then by the Baskerville family (members of whom were, incidentally, Quaker clothiers). It is now a hotel.

From about 1846 it was the residence of Captain Septimus Palairet. Palairet was a retired army officer who had married an American heiress. During his eight years in Bradford (he died in 1854), although he only had Woolley House on a twenty-one year lease he made substantial changes to it and also shifted the road from Woolley Hamlet to Woolley Green from outside his front door to its present route. He then renamed the building Woolley Grange. He also paid for the building of Christ Church School and helped finance the infant rubber industry which his friend Stephen Moulton had just started.

FRANKLEIGH HOUSE, Bath Road.

Frankleigh House as we see it today was the work of the Bailward family, Quaker clothiers become Methodists become landowners become Anglicans and, by marriage, become landed gentry.

Frankleigh House dates back in part to the early 1600s. The building was restored and extended in 1848 by the three unmarried daughters of Samuel Bailward of Horsington, Elizabeth, Julia and Amelia.

Before that the house had belonged to John Jones (died 1807). Jones had three sons, John, William and Leslie Grove. Son John built the large mill, now Nestle's, at Staverton in 1800 and became bankrupt in 1813.

Leslie Grove Jones (1779-1839) became in turn sailor, soldier and radical writer. As a teen-age ensign he left the Royal Navy in disgust at what he believed to have been an unjust flogging and joined the army, Lord Lansdowne having obtained for him a commission in the Guards Regiment, where in due course he rose to the rank of lieutenant colonel.

He fought in the Peninsular War and at Waterloo. On leaving the army he dedicated himself to party politics but his political ambitions seem to have been frustrated by lack of funds.

Immediately before John Jones owned it the house was run as a spa by Dr. Daniel Jones (no relation) hence, presumably, the later (temporary) style Kingswell Court . (Dr. Jones also conducted a spa at Holt, where Sawtell's bedding factory now stands.)

After the demise of the Bailward sisters the house became for a while a private so-called grammar school named Kingswell Court, then, until his death in 1917, the home of Canon the Honourable Sidney Meade (1839-1917), third son of the Earl of Clanwilliam. Canon Meade was for some years a curate of Christ Church, Bradford on Avon. He kept a large staff of domestic servants. In his *Memories of Bradford on Avon* Bertram Niblett relates that 'on Sundays the reverend gentleman would marshal both indoor and outdoor staff together, and dressed in their various uniforms they would be marched down the Bath Road to church for matins. Kitchen maids, cooks, coachmen, chambermaids...'

MIDWAY MANOR and the Shrapnel Family

The Shrapnels were Bradford clothiers from at least the seventeenth century. A stone tablet in Holy Trinity church records the deaths of Henry in 1688, three Zachariahs in 1723, 1761 and 1796, the Reverend Joseph in 1821 and General Henry Scrope Shrapnel in 1849.

The Old Manor House of Midway at Wingfield, three miles south of Bradford on the B3109, said to have dated from the twelfth century, was the boyhood home of General Henry Shrapnel, inventor of the exploding shell known by his name. The old house was pulled down and the present one built by Henry Summers Baynton in 1893.[10]

General Shrapnel

Henry Scrope Shrapnel was born in Bradford in 1761 and died on 13 March 1842. He was buried in the family vault in Holy Trinity church. (The year shown on the mural tablet is incorrect; a brass plate in the chancel floor records the correct one). He was the son of the Zachariah Shrapnel who died in 1796.

Henry Shrapnel was a regular officer in the Royal Artillery so keen on improving the efficiency of artillery bombardment that he devoted over many years his own time and money to it. The most effective and

107

Above: General Henry Shrapnel, inventor of the exploding ('shrapnel') shell.
(Photo: Ian Jones, National Army Museum).
Below: Midway Manor, Wingfield.

sinister of his inventions was the exploding shell. Shrapnel filled a metal canister or 'shell' with bullets and added a small bursting charge just sufficient to split it open at a given point, so that, instead of lobbing at the enemy a hunk of solid metal on a hit or miss basis, in future it would be possible to rain death and destruction all around. His claim for reimbursement of the small fortune he had spent fell on deaf ears, even in the light of a despatch from the Waterloo battlefield itself that the shell's deployment for the recapture of the key position at the farmhouse of La Haye Sainte, where the British line had been pierced, had been decisive.

Shrapnel had hoped that the government would reward and compensate him. All he got was a pension of £1200 a year, which he would have been better off without as he was passed over for promotion and the award was construed in such a way as to nullify other claims he had made for improving fire-power. There was talk of a baronetcy and the king was willing and ready; but Shrapnel seems to have been singularly lacking in friends in high places and nothing came of it. He left the army in 1825 and died at Southampton a very disgruntled man. His son, Henry Needham Scrope Shrapnel (1812-1896), after retirement in 1866 made it his business to press his father's claims but met with no greater success. Disenchanted with his native land he went to live in Canada.

On the stone piers of the gateway leading to the house are represented shrapnel bombs and the names of battles claimed to have been won by their use: Waterloo, Table Bay, Chuzneemedanse, Kioze, Bidasoa, Tsage and Busaco.

Midway Manor, with some 109 acres, was owned until his death in 1988 by Mr.Timothy Walker, United Kingdom chairman of the World Wildlife Fund. With his wife Rosemary he maintained there a private zoo of rare and exotic animals. The property was later owned for a while by Mr. Ronald Scott, chairman of the Caspian Pony Society, and his wife Jane. The present occupants are Mr. and Mrs. James Robson.

LEIGH HOUSE, NOW THE LEIGH PARK HOTEL,
Bradford Leigh

The house we see today was built in 1820 by Daniel Clutterbuck, a Bradford lawyer and banker, on the site of the sixteenth century property which he had acquired in 1789. Clutterbuck died in 1821 and the estate was sold to Admiral Fellowes. Fellowes (1778-1853), youngest son of Dr. William Fellowes, physician to George IV, came to Bradford on retirement after service with the East India Company and the Royal Navy. The next owner (from 1840) was the Reverend John Hopkins Bradney, the rich perpetual curate of Christ Church. After that it belonged to Miss Isabella Poynder, benefactress, as we have seen, of the Christ Church National School. From about 1880 to 1888 the estate was owned by Lady Jane Henrietta Swinburne, whose brother, the poet Charles Algernon Swinburne (1837-1909), is said to have stayed there for a time, and after that by Lord Fitzmaurice of Leigh.

During the Second World War Leigh House became a military hospital. From 1947 it was Bradford on Avon hospital. In 1979, the hospital having moved to Berryfield House, the property became the Leigh Park Hotel.

Leigh House, Bradford Leigh, now the Leigh Park Hotel.

Lord Fitzmaurice of Leigh

A very distinguished owner of Leigh House was Edmond George Petty-Fitmaurice (1846-1935), first Baron Fitzmaurice, second son of the fourth Marquis of Lansdowne, who lived there from 1890 till his death.

Fitzmaurice was Liberal Member of Parliament for Calne from 1868 to 1885, and from 1882 to 1885 was Under Secretary of State for Foreign Affairs in Gladstone's government. He was re-elected to parliament in 1898 as member for the North Division of Wiltshire. In 1905 he was elevated to the peerage as Lord Fitmaurice of Leigh, choosing his title from his home at Bradford Leigh.

Unlike his Tory elder brother, the fifth Marquis, who later became Viceroy of India, Fitzmaurice was a radical Liberal reformer, concerned for the underpaid and unenfranchised Wiltshire labouring classes and particularly interested in educational opportunity for all. It is known that many a young man in Wiltshire owed his university career to his unobtrusive generosity. He was a staunch advocate of reform of local government, land law, licensing law and the House of Lords, and a firm supporter of Home Rule for Ireland.

II "MADE AL OF STONE"

The streets are narrow and irregular; yet many good houses present themselves to the eye of the passenger.

The Universal British Directory 1793

Some good ones gone – and some saved

Bradford's charm is perennial. Streets and houses are as enjoyable now as they ever were. But some buildings that today we should save (often for fear of what might be put in their place!) have gone long since. At the corner where the church of St Thomas More (the former town hall) now stands once stood, as we know from an old print, a most attractive building; this may have been the inn called The Hare, It was demolished in 1854 to make way for the present building.

The earlier town hall (or market house as it was usually called) stood at the foot of Coppice Hill at the eastern end of the Shambles facing what is now number 32 Silver Street. Writing in the Wiltshire Archaeological Magazine in 1881 Canon Jones describes the building as it had been described to him by a resident who had known it as a boy. According to the Canon's informant:

The Old Market House was originally of what might be termed three storeys. The basement or cellar was on a level with the street opposite the shop now occupied by Mr Budget Jones the entrance joining the Royal Oak, and was used some 60 years ago as a crockery store. The second storey was an open colonnade looking up Coppice Lane and was full of butchers' stalls. The entrance was on the level of the Shambles and the storey itself consisted of three plain round columns one at each angle, between them being wooden palisading and a central column; to this last the ne'er-do-wells who were sentenced for some offence or other to have a whipping were bound. The third or upper storey consisted at one time of a room in which the courts were held and the business of the Manor transacted. But in my time (1820) it was in ruin and the staircase leading to it was gone. I remember, however, that it had three quaint projecting windows of a square-headed form, with thick deeply-moulded oak frames which were filled with small diamond panes of glass and looked into the Old Market Place. I remember the upper part falling down, whilst the lower was still, for some years afterwards, used by the butchers.

Canon Jones observed that against the wall of what was in his day the Royal Oak public house, (that is, the building at the east end of The Shambles on the south side) the lines of the roof gable might still be traced. They still can be. The building, long neglected in the protracted period of recession which, as described elsewhere, had begun around the turn of the century, in 1826 finally collapsed.

Another good building lost by neglect was the Wesleyan Chapel on Coppice Hill; its walls remain to remind us of what it once was. The row of shops in Market Street called Pippet Buildings would certainly have gone the same way and so might the Priory Barn in Newtown and Silver Street House; but all these were saved by the action of Bradford on Avon Preservation Trust.

Through the energy and initiative of the vicar, (the excellent Canon Jones again), St Catherine's Almshouses in Frome Road are still extant, (though probably nothing of the original building remains). The charity had been well-endowed. In 1702 it had possessed twelve and a half acres. But in 1834 the Charity Commissioners reported that as a result of gross misconduct on the part of the trustees more than half the land had passed to the ownership of either General Shrapnel or Sir John Hobhouse, with no record of payment. The only accounting the Charity Commissioners could find was in the banking books of Messrs. Hobhouse and Co – to whom the charity was in debt. The commissioners found the buildings in a deplorable state and reduced to three tenements, each of one floor with one almswoman.

In spite of this damning report things went on much as before for the next twenty-seven years. Then in 1861 the Charity Commissioners, prompted by Canon Jones, put things on a proper footing. In 1868 the almshouses were rebuilt (to the design of Bradford architect Charles Adye) as three new tenements, out of funds (£300) bequeathed by John Bubb. In 1878 the building was enlarged by the trustees to make one more tenement. Today there are three separate dwellings, two having been combined to make one. The trustees are the Lord of the Manor, the vicar of Holy Trinity church and two churchwardens.

The Hall's Almshouses in Frome Road, founded in AD 1700 by John Hall, have survived more or less in their original form thanks to benefactors, including the Duke of Kingston and, in the 1890s, Horatio Moulton who repaired and re-roofed them.

III BRADFORD ON AVON PRESERVATION TRUST

The wave of destruction which, triggered by the Housing Act of 1957, swept across the nation in the 1960s came early to Bradford, where the attractive terraces of seventeenth and eighteenth century stone cottages on the north-west slope of the town came under threat.

In December 1957 the Wiltshire Times reported a Bradford Urban District Council proposal to clear Tory, Middle Rank and Newtown of all existing buildings and erect council flats on the site. As a start, thirty-five houses on Tory and a number on Middle Rank were condemned. Outrage was national as well as local. In Bradford a preservation society (later to be reconstituted as the Bradford on Avon Preservation Trust) was formed with the declared object of maintaining the town's character, architectural interest and scenic qualities and, where new building was necessary, ensuring that it was in keeping.

In June 1963 the national media were able to report the success of the campaign to save the terraces. The local authorities had been won over. Not only had the District Council withdrawn the demolition order to allow a group of ten houses on Tory to be repaired, but the County Council had been a major contributor to the cost of so doing. Fired now with enthusiasm the District Council had purchased cottages on Middle Rank for similar treatment.

Though Bradford was spared the worst excesses of the decade by the energy and dedication of the Preservation Society and its supporters the town was not allowed to go entirely unscathed. The attractive stone-built former Quaker Meeting House which had stood in the town centre since 1718 was demolished and in 1965 a number of agreeable seventeenth century stone houses on St Margaret's Hill were pulled down to make way for council flats for the elderly. Vigorous efforts to secure a reprieve, supported by local and national media, had been in vain.

As time went on the Preservation Trust came to be accepted by the authorities as a responsible body whose opinion was worth seeking in planning matters and so, of more recent years, it has become able to exercise a restraining influence without confrontation. One instance of this was the saving from destruction of the Fitzmaurice Grammar School building in Junction Road after the school joined the Secondary Modern one to form St Laurence Comprehensive School.

The preservationists have not confined themselves to exhortation. To widen its scope the original Preservation Society has been reconstituted as an incorporated charitable body, Bradford on Avon Preservation Trust Ltd., with additional powers, among them the power to acquire property for the purpose of preserving it.

In the late 1960s the then derelict Priory Barn was bought by a member and presented to the Trust, who restored and converted it to its present use as an attractive centre for meetings and small social functions. (The architects were Hugh Roberts and Partners). In 1977 the late seventeenth century Silver Street House was renovated (architect R D Goodall); and in 1982 were rehabilitated, almost at the point of collapse, the row of shops in Market Street now called Pippet Buildings. This project received national acclaim and the 1984 Civic Trust Award. (The architects were Vernon Gibbs and Partners.) In 1992 the Trust rescued numbers 9, 10 and 11 Market Street. These were restored with the help of architects Niall Phillips and contractor Don Bailey.

NOTES

1. See also Canon J E Jackson's article, reprinted from the *Wiltshire Archaeological Magazine* on pages 232 to 236 of Canon Jones's History.

2. Wiltshire Archaeological Magazine Volume 5 pages 267-341.

3. This was the firm which during the severe industrial recession in 1841 failed and helped precipitate the failure of the bank of Hobhouse, Phillott and Lowder.

4. Mrs Barbara Harvey, a member of Wiltshire Buildings Record, tells me that she has identified the farmhouse called Maplecroft at Frankleigh (ST 82.3623) as having belonged to Thomas Rogers. Part of this ancient building remains as it was in his lifetime, thick walls, heavy joists and a fifteenth century doorway confirming a date of about 1500.

5. John Cam Hobhouse's friendship with the poet Byron was lifelong. Byron drew on the journey that they made together in Albania in his epic poem *Childe Harold; Journey through Albania* is Hobhouse's account. Canto IV of Childe Harold is dedicated to Hobhouse. Hobhouse's *Imitations and Translations from the Ancient and Modern Classics* contains nine poems by Byron.

6. Wiltshire Archaeological Magazine, Volume 41.

7. A coroner or clerk of the market was concerned with enforcement of the weights and measures laws and with fair dealing generally, particularly at markets and fairs. There will have been in Bradford as there was wherever fairs and markets were held, a court of *piedpoudre*. Canon Jones suggested that Pippet Street, the old name for Market Street, got its name from it. It seems likely. Pippet is as near to the French pronunciation as a Wiltshireman might want to get. (In Bristol, where, incidentally, the court, held before a recorder, still survives, they called it piepowder)

The court of *piedpoudre* was a very minor one, concerned with pedlars and petty chapmen – people with dusty feet. It settled disputes between buyer and seller on the spot; the complaint had to be made on the day the dispute arose and must be settled the same day.

8. WRO 1699/22.

9. *Memories of Bradford* on Avon by Bertram Niblett.

10. Ezekiel Edmonds, whose mills were in Church Street, was the last clothier member of a family who had been in the business in Bradford since at least 1791. We do not know a great deal about them and it may therefore be of interest to the genealogist or local historian that I chanced upon a descendant of theirs when I was living in the United States of America in the 1960s.

This was Major General James E Edmonds, a retired officer of the US National Guard, whose great-grandfather enlisted in the Royal Marines at Bradford on Avon on 9 September 1797 and, having served in the Napoleonic Wars, was entitled to a campaign medal but had never claimed it. The story was newsworthy at the time (February 1965) because General Edmonds, working on his family history, had enquired about the medal and was pleasantly surprised to be presented with it; his great-grandfather's entitlement had been confirmed by the Royal Marine Corps Records Office and the Royal Mint had struck one specially for him.

11. According to *Wiltshire and Dorsetshire at the Opening of the 20th Century* published in 1906 in Pike's New Century Series.

7.

EVERYDAY LIFE
DOWN THE YEARS

Iron Age Bradfordians: the settlement on Budbury.

The modest digs of 1969 and 1986 proved the existence of a substantial Iron Age settlement. We are unlikely, now, ever to learn more about these earliest inhabitants, but from finds elsewhere in the county (displayed to excellent effect in Devizes Museum) we can conjecture something of their way of life.

Until the present century, Iron Age Celts were called vaguely 'Ancient Britons' and thought of as uncivilised and uncouth. Wiltshireman John Aubrey pictured them as 'almost as savage as the beasts, whose skins were their only raiment'; he will have got this from the account by Julius Caesar which so described the Cantii warriors who foiled his first attempt to invade Britain in 55 BC.

Caesar must have known that the truth was very different. Unlike him (who wrote and published his own version of events) the ancient Celts, alas, did not write histories. From more serious Roman historians, such as Tacitus, we know that they were doughty defenders of their homelands, but, until modern archaeologists got to work, we knew relatively little about their way of life. From them we now know that Iron Age Celts farmed and bred stock, ploughed the land with iron ploughshares and reaped with iron sickles. They kept ponies, pigs, cows, oxen, sheep and possibly goats. They ate the pigs, milked the cows and used the oxen for transport. Above all, and probably most profitably, like their successors hereabouts, they kept sheep, milked them, ate their flesh and, using spindle whorls of pottery, spun their wool then wove it on looms equipped with loom-weights of baked clay.

They manufactured a wide range of metal tools and weapons, made domestic pottery, were efficient carpenters and lived in houses. They made leather and used it for clothes, belts, ropes, bags and thongs. In their homes they used a wide range of implements made from animal bone; knife handles, bodkins, buttons and even razors have been found – in the museum at Devizes there is an Iron Age one made of bronze. In various places stores of clay sling-shots have been found, evidently kept handy for use for offence or defence.

Iron Age folk were traders and had a coinage. Many of their coins have been found in our part of Wiltshire, notably at Box, Yatton Keynell and Minety. Coins were of gold, silver and bronze and from at least the first century BC were struck here. We know of Iron Age settlements at North Wraxall and Castle Combe and many other places.

The Budbury community was a small one, probably one or two inter-related families, living in a forest clearing. We do not know exactly when it settled there or for how long. But it was probably still there when the Romans came – farming, growing wheat, barley, oats and rye and living warmly clothed in woollens in round houses of stone or strongly-con-structed timber framework with wattle-work walls and cone-shaped roofs of thatch, rushes or turves, baking their bread and cooking their meat, keeping bees, brewing mead and beer and talking a language very much like modern Welsh.

The Romano-British.

Romans settled around Budbury in about the first century AD, probably not long after Bath was first garrisoned. There is also evidence of Roman occupation elsewhere in the town. Besides the coins and other artefacts found at Priory House (see Chapter 6), Dr Doreen Ellis found in her garden in St Margaret's Street in 1987 a piece of Roman glass; and Miss Joan Ward uncovered in her garden at Southleigh a short length of wall which very strongly suggested a Roman origin. In the grounds of the nearby Barge Inn a fragment of Roman hypocaust is said to have been unearthed. The discovery at Budbury in 1976 of the bath-house of a Roman or Romano-British villa showed that Bradford on Avon Romans lived in some style, as top Romans and their British imitators customarily did.

The Saxons.

The first Saxon Bradfordians settled on the south side of the river. Like their fellows elsewhere they will have lived simply, in small wooden buildings, sleeping on the floor or on a bench on a sack of straw. They customarily built in wood and the original Saxon church here may well have been of that material, to be rebuilt later in the excellent stone available in abundance.

For transport haulage and ploughing, Saxons, canny and practical, preferred oxen to horses. They were cheaper to feed, they could be milked and eaten, and they were less likely than horses to be taken for war. Oxen were central to Saxon culture. They beat out tracks and served to measure land; a hide, which could be anything from forty to a hundred acres, depending on the terrain, was the area a team of oxen and one ploughman could plough in a season.

Saxons tended to shun life in towns, and up to the time of the Norman conquest there were probably more families living in isolated farmsteads in the vicinity than in Bradford on Avon itself. The existence of the abbey or monastery founded by Aldhelm in the late seventh or early eighth century probably added significantly to a town population then measured in low three figures; and given that most Bradfordians then will still have been worshipping trees there must have been substantial cultural and religious input by the time, three centuries later, the monastery was destroyed by Danish raiders. While the monastery existed there may have been some very basic medical care. After its destruction there will have been little or nothing.

In Norman times.

The Norman conquest brought progress and stability. In the 1200s the town acquired the solid stone bridge we still have, and it had a hospital again. True that it was only a leper hospital – St Margaret's. But the presence of a lazar house (as such places were called, after the biblical Lazarus) is significant of Bradford's importance. By the fourteenth century lazar houses existed in every town of any size. The spread of the disease probably had to do with trade, domestic and international, and woollen material was probably a classic carrier. Lazar houses were built and endowed as charities but were rather more for the protection of the local populace than for the relief of the victim. A suspected leper was subject to examination by the parish priest and a jury. If found infected, he or she was required to wear distinctive clothing, including, for a man a hood, for a woman a double veil. Thereafter they were subject to strict rules of conduct and social intercourse. In Bristol in the fourteenth century they enacted laws for the expulsion of lepers; in Bradford on Avon they seem to have been less harsh.

Change, administrative and cultural, came about gradually. Something like the feudal system had existed even before the Norman conquest. The Abbess of Shaftesbury had held the manor of Bradford from AD 1001 and continued to hold it on the same terms after the Norman takeover. Within a century a grand parish church was built in stone, but for a very long time after that houses and cottages were of timber[1] with thatched roofs. Such stone buildings as were built were roofed with split stone tiles of forest marble, a hard slaty stone found here and there in Bradford on Avon among the softer jurassic oolite, specifically, as John Leland noted when he visited in the 1540s, at Budbury.

As time went on, Bradford on Avon, not adversely affected by the Norman Conquest and the later struggle for power between the barons and the king, prospered greatly. As early as the 1200s the town had a clothing industry. We have seen that in 1249 Adam the Fuller operated a fulling-mill by water-power. We also know, in the same century, of Nicholas the Dyer.

The later Middle Ages and thereafter.

In Norman times the standard of living was higher than before, though, for most, still basic. Furniture for most homes was minimal, a table, a bench and a bed, the bed a couch-like wooden object often combined with a chest.

From the earliest times, fish from the river, or even specially bred, was a valuable source of protein. Eels abounded. The earliest occupants of Chantry House in Church Street, the chantry priests, doubtless made good use of the capacious built-in stone tank, to this day kept permanently replenished by a hillside spring, the water entering at one side and flowing out at the other. In the monastic tradition the earliest occupants probably used this not only for keeping fish fresh for the table but also for breeding them; monasteries customarily had what was called a 'stew pond' for breeding carp and other fish.

Pigeons and their eggs were a valuable supplement to diet. For many centuries it was only the lord of the manor, and, with his permission, the parson, who could build a dovecote to encourage pigeons. Barton Farm had one in the Middle Ages, when it was the manor house, and we know where it must have been; nearby Culver Close derives its name from the Anglo-Saxon word *culfre*, a dove or pigeon.

The Normans introduced rabbits to England and Conigre Hill (see later) is a reminder of what folk like Adam le Folur and Nicholas the Dyer might have enjoyed for dinner. The swans that we see on the river Avon today may well be the descendants of those which belonged as of right to the medieval lord of the manor. At Barton Farm they were included in the Shaftesbury Abbey accounts in a list of domesticated farm animals. The abbess of Shaftesbury doubtless enjoyed on special occasions (as a change from boar's head) a dish of swan. It was customary to pluck the bird and cook it whole, impaled on a spit, then bring it, dressed in its feathers, ceremoniously to the table with a piece of blazing camphor on a wick in its beak.

In the Middle Ages vegetables were not widely used, but herbs and spices were. In large households there was always a herb garden for cooking and physic. Very important were saffron, tansy, sage and samphire. Honey was the only sweetener until sugar was introduced after the crusades. There was also frumenty (hulled wheat boiled in milk and seasoned with cinnamon and honey), gingerbread and sillabub (a dish made with milk or cream mixed with wine into soft curd).

Adam the fuller and Nicholas the dyer will have had their rabbit served on a trencher. Trenchers (or tranchoirs) were the original dinner-plate. At first they were thick slices of coarse bread, made out of meal, as it came, unrefined, from the mill. They could either be eaten after the food placed upon them or thrown into an alms-basket, with other leavings, for the poor. Later on, trenchers became square pieces of wooden board and for many centuries remained in that form as standard items of domestic equipment.

Diet and eating habits have always had everything to do with income, fashion, and station in life. Rich Roman Bradfordians will have eaten venison and pork but will have preferred poultry. Poorer ones will have eaten bacon. Medieval and Tudor Englishmen were substantial meat-eaters and the better-off Bradfordians will have consumed large amounts of flesh of all kinds, in particular roast beef. The less well-off will have subsisted on what they happened to be able to afford, which might be salt beef or bacon, supplemented by the occasional rabbit or hare. A typical meal for a clothworker's family then will have been bread, bacon, milk-whey and beer.

In the households of the gentry (The Hall, the Manor House, Rogers's – later called Methuen's – and perhaps the vicarage) in the Middle Ages the day probably begun with a glass of beer and a piece of bread. The main meal of the day will have been between nine and eleven o'clock in the morning and there will have been a lighter one between four and six in the afternoon.

Later on (sixteenth century) Bradford gentry will have dined at eleven o'clock in the morning and, as was then the practice for their class, have taken their time over it, perhaps as much as three hours. They will have taken their second and final meal at about six o'clock in the evening. Middle ranking Bradfordians such as clothiers, merchants and farmers will have dined at noon and supped between seven and eight o'clock in the evening.

Up at the Hall in the eighteenth century the Duke of Kingston and Elizabeth Chudleigh will have taken early morning tea instead of beer and their breakfast may have included oysters. A light snack at noon will have been followed by a heavy dinner between two and three in the afternoon. Late afternoon tea will have been followed by supper at about nine in the evening.

At the beginning of the nineteenth century dinner-time for fashion-able people will have been between four and five in the afternoon. By mid-century it had slipped to between six and seven, with a light lunch between one and two, and tea between three and five. At the other end of the social scale working people continued to eat the main meal at midday.

Hygiene and health

For a good many people Bradford on Avon has for the past two and a half thousand years consistently been a good place in which to live and work.

If, however, we were suddenly whisked back to any earlier age in the town's history we should not like it. For one thing we should object to the dirt everywhere. Although, from the Middle Ages on, the law required each householder in town to keep the area outside his house clean and clear, and the better-off employed street sweepers to do it, for the most part streets were filthy; Bradfordians relied on rain, and the town's many natural watercourses, to wash garbage, horse-dung and cattle-droppings

In Newtown, new in the late seventeenth century days of industrial revival.

down to the river, itself already looked upon by inhabitants and industry as a sewer provided free of charge by bountiful nature. As late as 1867, the *Post Office Directory of Dorsetshire, Wiltshire and Hampshire* could complacently record:

> Bradford is considered to be a very pleasing, exceedingly picturesque and very healthy town, well defended from the north and east winds, while its situation is such that all its impurities, after passing down its sloping streets, are immediately carried off by the waters of the Avon.

Dirt gave rise to sickness. Bubonic plague (the so-called Black Death of 1348), for some reason notoriously high among weavers, struck again twice in the seventeenth century.

In the Quarter Sessions Records we read that in 1609:

> The town of Bradford petition for relief, having been for 20 weeks infected with the plague, and the tax imposed upon places within five miles of the town proving insufficient for relief of the infection, the Justices ordered that Chippenham, Melksham and Whorwellsdown Hundreds should be assessed to contribute.

There was a further outbreak in 1646. The authorities did not connect the disease with the existence of rats who carried the disease and spread it through their fleas, the fleas themselves thriving in dust and dirt. (Such conditions were not peculiar to small towns like Bradford on Avon; in 1741 the streets of London were described by one writer as 'abounding with such heaps of filth as a savage would look on with amazement'.)

Fleas and lice proliferated. Wooden beds, bed-bug friendly, continued in general use up to and well beyond the time of the industrial revolution and were usually infested. (It was not until the middle of the last century that a Bristol man, Francis Augustus Barnett, invented the iron bedstead.) There were regular smallpox epidemics right up to the beginning of the present century. Methodist preacher Thomas Olivers, who was himself near to death with the disease in 1752, later wrote that in that particular epidemic 'scarce a single person escaped and six or seven a night were buried in Bradford alone'. Though things were not quite as bad as that, they were bad enough. Canon Jones's history of the town states that from July 1752 to May 1753 189 died. 1267 are said to have recovered. The population was probably then about five thousand, so about one in three caught the disease.

We do not know just when the hospital John Leland mentioned when he visited the town in the 1540s ceased to exist. But it is safe to say that for the ensuing centuries up to our own there was nothing remotely resembling one. This was to change largely through the enterprise and initiative of local businessman Albert William Davis, who bought Leigh House when it came on the market in 1936 and held it, and maintained the grounds at his own expense, for two years until the local hospital committee felt able to take it over. But by this time the project was overtaken by events. War was imminent, and the hospital became a military one until after hostilities ceased. In 1947 Bradford on Avon at last got its hospital. It remained at Leigh House until 1979, when it moved to Berryfield House.

Given the hard slog involved in 'doing the washing' it is not surprising that shirts and underclothes went unlaundered for very much longer than we would tolerate today. In the big houses it was customary to do the laundry every two or three months. This was a major exercise involving outside washerwomen as well as domestic staff. A reminder of those days and ways is Bertram Niblett's recollection of seeing in Woolley Street, as a boy in the early years of this century, the laundry of The Hall with 'steam pouring from the wooden vents in the wall of the upper storey'. Up to at least the beginning of the nineteenth century clothes were washed in the river, the usual place being the slips below the town bridge.

The privy in the cottage backyard, often shared with the neighbours, housed one bucket which served the vegetable garden and another the needs of the clothing industry. The latter contained a saleable commodity. Right up to the end of the nineteenth century human urine was used to dissolve the natural oil (lanolin) in the wool. The product was put out in jars supplied by the clothiers and collected in the sig-cart, a two-wheeled barrow with an arched rod across it, from which a tub was suspended.

At the workhouse sig was carefully salvaged by the authorities and sold to set off against the cost of maintaining the poor. Workhouse sig was claimed to be of superior quality for its purpose because the principle component of a pauper's diet was skilly.

The Public Health Act of 1875 compelled water companies to provide a constant supply of water to towns, but piped water did not come to Bradford on Avon till 1883. It would have come sooner had Bradford folk's pride, and their hostility to their old rival Trowbridge, not caused them to reject the Trowbridge Water Company's offer to supply them, too.

Before that, all water was drawn by hand from the well, if you were sufficiently well-placed to have one, or carried from one or other of the public fountains fed by mountain streams (such as Ladywell in Newtown or Pippett's pump in Market Street) if you were not. In *Memories of Bradford on Avon* Bertram Niblett tells how his grandmother, in about the 1850s, carried water from Pippett's Pump up the hill to the house on Tory where she worked as a servant[2].

Pumps and wells were in general use well into the present century (one existed at the Hall's Almshouse until piped water was installed in 1957). When piped water came, only the better off had it indoors. For others there were street standpipes, in use within living memory. They were located in Bridge Street, Bullpit, Whitehill, Bath Road, Winsley Road and other places. A characteristic of towns like Bradford on Avon, when town water came, was the installation of horse troughs and/or drinking fountains in main thoroughfares. Bradford's stood in Market Street, in front of the Swan Hotel, but for only a few years. It was put there by the Dainton family in 1919 to the memory of Lieutenant Howard Hillier Dainton and his comrades killed in the first world war, but removed in 1932, regarded by that time as an obstruction to traffic.

Snuffy Bradford

With the changeover from water-power to steam, the central part of the town, in particular the parts adjacent to the river banks, will have been smoky and sometimes beset by fog. Many of the buildings were run down and the area slummy. Those without a specific reason to stay and who could afford to live elsewhere in the town did so. In 1851 when Canon Jones came to take up his living, he found the Holy Trinity church largely abandoned by the upper crust in favour of Christ Church, and the building showing clear signs of neglect. An official report on the nearby free grammar school (now Trinity Church Hall) described it as being 'in a bad part of the town'.

The area on the east bank was, if anything, even more run down. An official report of 1880 describes what it was like in the vicinity of St Margaret's Hall, alongside which the British School was housed in the long disused Quaker Meeting House. A Board of Education inspector recommended that the school be closed because of 'the unsavoury surroundings'. Part of St Margaret's Street does, however, seem to have preserved its respectability, to judge by the 1881 census return. Business-man George Spencer, of Spencer, Moulton and Co., brewers, lived at Westbury House with his wife and daughter and three domestic servants. Herbert Applegate 'woollen cloth manufacturer employing 250 persons' lived near by in St Margaret's Street with his wife and family of seven children and two domestic servants.

Was it the smoky atmosphere of the town rather than the brief presence of a snuff mill that gave rise to the epithet 'snuffy' applied derisively to Bradford on Avon by, according to Daniel Batchelor (see below), natives of Bath? The term 'snuff' will have been familiar in the days when a standard piece of household equipment was a metal 'snuffer', used to crop the carbon which formed on the candle wick in days when candles were crudely manufactured and smoked a good deal[2].

In Georgian Times

I am grateful to Jack Stafford, Bradfordian born and bred, for lending me a reprint, handed down to him by his father, of an account which appeared in the *North Wilts Mercury* in 1885, entitled *Reminiscences of Bradford 50 Years Ago, by an Old Bradfordian in America*.

Writing from Utica, New York, Daniel Batchelor gives a flamboyant account life in Bradford on Avon not long after Waterloo.

One of his earliest memories was the roasting of an ox whole at the back of 'Seal's buildings on Trowbridge Road' on the occasion of the coronation of George IV, on 19 July 1821.

Nonconformist churches of his day were remembered, and the idio-syncrasies and their ministers recounted with glee. At Lady Huntingdon's Chapel a feature was 'my lady's majestic coat of arms, which was nearly six feet square, painted white and posted in front of the pulpit before the humble congregation as a sort of awful insignia of something or other'.

The magistrates of the day were Thomas Saunders and Thomas Tugwell, the latter so diminutive that he could be taken for a boy were it not for his 'fine leonine face'.

Ma'am Dolls or Doles kept a dame school on Coal Ash Walk, above Chantry, but did not succeed in teaching young Daniel the alphabet.

The more enterprising clothiers were going ahead with steam and machinery. The first Boulton and Watts engine in the town was installed by Posthumus Bush in his factory on Whitehill, 'Old Posey', as they called him, 'would walk about the barton in female pattens when the weather was nasty'.

He remembered when the 'tithemen put up the new stocks on Whitehill in accordance with the statute of Edward III' but did not remember that they were ever used. There was 'clipping the church at Shrovetide' and there were noisy skimmertons and jolly wassailers. (For more about these customs and practices see Chapter 11.) Public health and hygiene were not paramount; chitterlings were washed at Lady Well and clothes laundered in the river and banged with 'bwitles' on the 'slips below Bradford bridge'. Street vendors cried their wares with piercing voice – water-cress, hot cakes, sand and fine mackerel; donkey-drivers hawked sacks of coal.

Trinity Fair (held in Church Street) was a great occasion. There were gingerbread stalls all the way along from the Swan Inn to Edmonds's factory and nearly up to the 'baish' on Pippett (now Market) Street. 'Old Thespian Lismore, with his bespangled corps, came annually to it and pitched his tent in the new market place' (outside the Swan), while over the bridge would come Wombwell or Atkins with 'blaring bands, roaring beasts and flaring canvas pictures, which last were hauled into place amid the applause of the noisy multitude'. The cattle and horse fairs extended from Timbrells (by St Margaret's Hall) up to the old poorhouse (it stood where the cutting made for the railway station now is).

From Batchelor's account of an election campaign in 1837 it seems that early Victorian Bradford on Avon and Dickens's Eatenswill had much in common. The contest for the Devizes seat was between Wiltshireman Paul Methuen, sponsored by Sir John Cam Hobhouse, and Sir Francis Burdett[4]. A rowdy election meeting in the market place was broken up by Burdett's 'bludgeon men'. Batchelor fled with the 'motley crowd' of Bradford on Avon men and boys and claimed that he did not stop till he reached 'that abode of the quiet Quakers called, in the dialect, 'Milsom' (Melksham).

Batchelor continues:

The wrath of Bradford was terrible, an indignation meeting was held at The Swan, and the bludgeon men, together with Burdett who set them on, were denounced in idioms and in adjectives peculiar to the inhabitants of North Wilts. On the platform the bludgeon men were declared to be lawless ruffians... Jack Hibberd's mutton pies, Old Forth's baked faggots and Mother Haswell's black puddings were incontinently devoured by the roarers and huge pots of swipes (small beer) were given to those who roared the loudest at the headquarters of the opposing candidates. Great was the seething commotion, neighbours disputing with neighbours...sometimes Ezekiel Edmonds, elegant in form and fiery in action would stir up the Reformers till the old club-rooms would reverberate his eloquent words "How dare this Westminster renegade, this hoary old turncoat, to ask for the votes of the electors of North Wiltshire?"

NOTES

1.See Wiltshire Archaeological Magazine volume 86 (1993) pages 126/8. The article by R B and B K Harvey Bradford on Avon in the fourteenth century based on a careful analysis of the accounts of Shaftesbury Abbey for the manor of Bradford is invaluable for the period.

2. Such tasks had their dangers. In July 1819 a local newspaper reported that:

> Between nine and ten o'clock on Monday night as a young woman was going along one of the principal streets in Bradford with a can of water on her head, she was met by a man called John Hodgson, a stonemason, who, being intoxicated, began to take liberties with her.

Mrs Wainwright, aged nearly seventy, who intervened, was struck twice by Hodgson so hard that she died a few hours later.

3. My grandmother used a snuffer and I still have it. It is constructed rather like a pair of scissors, one blade of which 'snuffed' the candle. The other blade comprises a metal box into which the 'snuff' was automatically consigned and trapped to retain smoke and smell.

When Canon Jones took up his post as the new vicar of Holy Trinity church, he found the building lit by 'simple dips, which, of a winter evening, just made darkness visible'. The dips needed constant attention and creaking snuffers made a sound which the canon found at times distracting. He observed that 'the poorer folk used a similar apparatus for snuffing dips'. (Dips were wicks dipped in melted tallow.)

4. Sir Francis Burdett (1770-1844) had been a leading Radical politician all his life until then, an advocate of parliamentary reform who denounced the war with France, flogging in the armed forces and corruption in parliament. He was imprisoned twice (in 1810 and 1820) on political charges. He had been Radical Member of Parliament for Westminster from 1807 until, following the Reform Act of 1832, he turned Tory and in 1837 successfully contested the North Wilts constituency seat as a Conservative.

8.
LOCAL GOVERNMENT

The concept of an elected local authority was unknown until the nineteenth century. In Bradford on Avon, as elsewhere, administrative and judicial authority grew out of those two once all-powerful bodies, the Church and the manor house. Links between the two were invariably close; in some places manorial courts were held in the parish church and the manorial records kept there. The parish, the district from which the local church drew its congregation was the area governed, and the vestry, under the vicar, was the unit of government. It survived as such, still symbolising the authority of the established church and meeting under its aegis until almost the end of the nineteenth century. Its authority was curtailed by the Bradford Town Improvement Act of 1839, but it was not until 1894 that it ceased altogether to have local government powers.

In its heyday the vestry comprised the vicar and about a score of the most influential parishioners selected by him. In the eighteenth century, for example, we find in the vestry minutes the names of such well-known Bradford on Avon clothiers as John Shrapnel, Paul Methuen, Francis Yerbury, Henry Methuen and Humphrey Tugwell. The vestry met once a month and was served by the parish clerk. Originally concerned almost exclusively with the cost of maintaining the fabric of the parish church, for which they were empowered to levy 'church rates' on property-owners,(of whom in Bradford on Avon in 1730 there were 134) the vestry's responsibilities gradually evolved as a form of local government.

The church building needed to be protected against fire. This called for fire-fighting equipment and trained men ready at short notice to operate it. So we have the beginnings of a town fire brigade, with a team made up of the bell-ringers as the original firemen. The vestry purchased fire buckets and a fire engine and paid for its maintenance. The fire engine was a tank and hand-pump on wheels. Its flexible leather hose was kept supple by regular oiling, as we know from payments shown in the accounts. It was kept in the churchyard.

Attendance at fires elsewhere in the parish was accepted as a public duty. Five shillings was paid by the vestry for 'playing the engine' (presumably fire practice and general testing of equipment) and this was the usual charge when the engine was called out to private property, though it could be as much as a guinea (21 shillings). The accounts do not show any repayments by beneficiaries and this doubtless justified and encouraged the additional voluntary contributions called for; a vestry minute of April 1730 records voluntary contributions amounting to £66 'for the purchasing of engines to extinguish fires ... for the preservation of the church from any fire that may appear'.

Acts of Parliament imposed duties on the vestry, for example in relation to the poor (see Chapter 10) and in respect of 'vermin'. Acts of Parliament of 1532/3 and 1566 called for the suppression of such 'vermin' as hedge-hogs, owls and other creatures deemed harmful to man, and parish vestries had to award for evidence of destruction.[1]

As lay responsibilities grew, parish church affairs gradually became less significant. Nonconformity thrived in the town and vestrymen and churchwardens no longer necessarily belonged to the established church. (The neglected state of Holy Trinity church building when Canon Jones arrived in 1851, described elsewhere, reflects this.) But in the eighteenth century, as contemporary vestry accounts show, spending connected with Holy Trinity church was readily approved.

Maintenance of the church bells and the striking mechanism of the church clock were important because the clock has no face. The chimes also called for regular expenditure. And the vestry were proud of their organ and ready to lavish money on it. There were also unexpected expenses. On Sunday 14 October 1759 there was a commotion in church. The Reverend Mr Glynn Clark was 'by threats deterred and by force hindered from performing divine service'. There was 'insulting language and many other disorders and misdemeanours as well by strangers as parishioners', as a result of which churchwarden Thomas Rogers was instructed to take the offenders to court at the parish cost. (See Chapter 9 for the general unruliness and open contempt for authority then current.)

Sometimes there were little windfalls. In 1737 the authorities swooped on forty-four keepers of unlicensed ale-houses and fined them a total of £3.

Staffing was minimal. It comprised principally churchwardens, ccnstables, overseers of the poor and the surveyor of roads, all of whom were unpaid; the parish clerk, the sexton, the coroner (or clerk) of the market and the town crier were remunerated. They were all appointed by the vestry. Operating in parallel with the vestry, but also at county level were the unpaid Justices of the Peace, with powers both judicial and administrative.

Churchwardens were important people in the local hierarchy. From the Middle Ages up to the end of the late nineteenth century their duties extended beyond the care of the parish church. From the sixteenth century on, they were responsible for, among other things, supervising pedlars, testing ale, controlling vermin, providing malt for brewing church ales (see later) and testing the ale when brewed, assisting in the administration of the Poor Law (until 1892 they were *ex officio* overseers of the poor) and road repairs and maintenance. Some offices were undertaken with great reluctance. Apart from the occasional Dogberry, nobody wanted to be a constable.

Overseers of the poor were appointed to distribute the money derived from the Poor Rate, to organise employment and to make themselves responsible for the poor-house.

The surveyor was a local business man who took his turn to see that the statutory obligation to keep local roads in repair was carried out.

Up to the Reformation the parish clerk was usually a clergyman, after that always a layman. The name of the parish and vestry clerk best known to us is that of Edward Orpin (died 1781), whom we have already met. Orpin served the vestry and was paid for so doing. His duties varied, from seeing that church laundry was attended to, to tackling, on the vicar's behalf, Quakers who had refused to pay tithe and church rates.

In June 1786 the shortcomings of sexton Silas Brown gave rise to a vestry minute reminding him of a sexton's duties. He must attend church on Sunday, and be present at all other services such as christenings, thanksgivings and funerals, in order to ensure that good order was maintained and sobriety observed. He must stay sober himself. (As it turned out, his days as sexton were numbered. A few days later Silas Brown has gone, having been charged with 'a very serious crime'.)

The coroner of the market was responsible for checking weights and measures and ensuring fair dealing in the market.

In days when few could read, the town crier performed an essential public service. He 'cried' public meetings, stolen property (surplices in

Where The Shambles, Silver Street and Coppice Hill meet was where the old town hall and market house stood till it collapsed in 1826 for want of maintenance. It served as a place for public punlishment, complete with whipping-post, stocks and pillory.

1804), warnings against misbehaviour on church premises such as gaming (1795) and fives play (1799). The office of town crier, as a serious public service, was still extant in 1867, as is shown by official directories of that year when the incumbent was George Stevens, who was also a green-grocer in The Shambles. In 1881 the town crier was Edward Melksham, who lived in Bridge Street. The town crier was paid for his services as they were required; according to Daniel Batchelor they might include advertising.

That still surviving medieval relic, the unpaid magistracy, was at the height of its power in the seventeenth and eighteenth centuries. It was in 1361 that local lords and gentry, as conservators of the peace, were first given wide powers, which they hung on to until nearly the end of the nineteenth century. In theory the Justices of the Peace were royal appointees, as they are today. In practice they chose each other with the co-operation of the Lord Lieutenant of the County. The name Methuen appears often. Magistrates were the really powerful ones in local government and, though unpaid, welcomed the opportunity to act in the interests of their class. Their administrative duties were increased from Tudor times on.

In the nineteenth century reform was in the air. The system of election to parliament was overhauled by the Reform Act of 1832, which gave the vote to the middle classes, thereby increasing the electorate nationwide from about 478,000 to about 814,000. Improved communications increasingly brought central government surveillance. A radical change in local government was effected by the Bradford Town Improvement Act of 1839. In future the government was to be by a body of nominated townsmen, called commissioners, who must reside within two miles and be property-owners. Future vacancies were to be filled by majority vote of ratepayers. The area to be governed was a circle of a radius of one mile from the Swan Inn. The commissioners were empowered to levy a rate for paving, lighting, cleaning, draining, policing and the maintenance of the fire brigade. They could enforce sanitary regulations and even had some rudimentary town-planning powers in the case of unsatisfactory building.

The Reform Act of 1867 extended the franchise further to include, in the counties, leaseholders and copyholders of property valued at £5 per annum and occupiers of property rated at £12; in the boroughs it enfranchised all householders and rentpayers of £10 per annum. The urban working classes now had the vote, and, in 1884, agricultural labourers who were householders were given it too. The scene was set for radical change. In 1894 the Bradford Town Improvement Act was superseded by the Local Government Act. Thereafter local government was to be by elected county councils assisted by elected district councils and the magistrates' administrative powers were confined to the licensing laws and the visiting of prisons and mental hospitals.

*Bradford on Avon Library, opened in June 1990, photographed
on market day (Thursdays)*

NOTE

1. They would pay for the killing of sparrows (threepence for a dozen severed heads),
foxes (one shilling per corpse), hedgehogs (threepence), polecats (threepence), otters (one
shilling), adders (one shilling). 'martin cats' (sixpence). (A 'martin cat' was, I think, the
furry catsized mammal that we would nowadays call a marten.) This law remained in
force until the latter part of the last century.

Today hedgehogs, once seen as a scourge, are not merely tolerated but actively
encouraged and protected. There is even a hedgehog preservation society. A letter in *The
Times* newspaper of 6 March 1990 from Mr A H Coles, founder of it, congratulated road-
builders on providing underground pedestrian crossings for them...

9.
KEEPING THE PEACE

Courts of Law

From the town's earliest days justice was administered in the two manorial courts, the court baron and the court leet. Both were held under the authority of the lord of the manor and both were partly administrative and partly judicial. In Bradford on Avon the lord of the manor, from the year 1001, was the abbess of Shaftesbury. Deputising for her, and based at Barton Farm, the manor house, was the steward of the manor, answerable to her for good management and also dispensing justice in the manorial courts.

The court baron was normally held once or twice a year and dealt with disputes between individuals in respect of debts, claims for damage and disagreements relating to lands within the manor. The court might be held at any place within the manor on fifteen days notice. Cases were dealt with be-fore freeholders of the manor and only freeholders could sue.

The court leet was held under royal charter. It originated under the Saxon kings and its original purpose was to call young men together to swear allegiance to the Crown. It developed into a minor criminal court for trial by jury of petty offences, indictments to higher courts and local civil disputes (usually over land ownership). In due course it developed into a formal court presided over by the steward of the leet, who had the powers and status of a judge. In the fourteenth century the courthouse seems to have been located in the vicinity of the Saxon church[1]. It may well have been meeting there, or not far away, from the days of Alfred the Great. Later on, for many centuries, the court leet met in the town hall which stood at the corner of the Shambles and Coppice Hill and which, long out of use and badly neglected, collapsed in 1826.

Policing

Before 1839, crime prevention was haphazard and the maintenance of law and order patchy.

An early official with what might be called police powers was the hayward, elected and sworn in at the court baron. The hayward's duty was to look after the boundary fences and keep animals from trespassing on common pasture enclosed for grass-growing. At night he had to be on the lookout for petty thieves[2]. He also had to round up labour for haymaking and harvest duties.

The bailiff of the manor, reponsible for overall management, also had some judicial powers, as did the reeve who served under him.

The Statute of Winchester of 1285 required every town or village to appoint in rotation two or more able-bodied householders to serve from Ascension Day to Michaelmas to watch from dusk to dawn and to arrest strangers. The watch served under the petty constable. The statute remained in force up to 1827.

By the eighteenth century Justices of the Peace were the real power in town and county, both in the matter of local government and in criminal jurisdiction. Petty sessions were held in Bradford on Avon from at least 1722. Magistrates of the hundred[3] appointed a high constable to ensure the keeping of the peace throughout it. Petty constables were nominated by the vestry and sworn in by the magistrates. Their duty was to maintain good order, apprehend and whip beggars and delinquents and to 'raise hue and cry'. (Raising hue and cry was defined as 'pursuit with horn and voice felons and such as have dangerously wounded another'). Petty constables were untrained, unpaid and usually unwilling; they might be assisted by part-time special constables, usually local tradesmen, who wore an armband and carried a stave. (Shakespeare, it will be remembered, immortalised their kind as Dogberry, Verges and the Watch in *Much Ado about Nothing*.)

There was also the sheriff's posse – the *posse comitatus* – literally the power of the county, which consisted of able-bodied males above the age of fifteen. All except peers and clergy were liable to serve at the summons of the sheriff of the county to defend the county against the enemies of the Crown or to keep the peace or to pursue felons or to enforce the royal writ. Failure to obey the summons incurred fine and imprisonment. The posse fell into disuse with the establishment of the county police force in 1839.

Punishment

Depending on the social status of the accused and the offence the court punished minor breaches of the law with imprisonment, fine, stocks, cucking-stool or pillory.

A spell in the stocks was commonly the penalty for petty offences by working men. The form of punishment dates back to Saxon times, so it is a fair assumption that stocks were in use in Bradford on Avon from the earliest days of the court leet[4]. They customarily stood in the most public place – the market place, the village green, the parish churchyard. In Bradford on Avon they were at one time adjacent to the market-hall at the bottom of Coppice Hill. Later they were moved to the southern end of the town bridge. Daniel Batchelor (see Chapter 7) recalled new stocks being set up on Whitehill in the 1830s.

There was also the pillory and a whipping-post. From the town's earliest days they will have been located in the market place. Later on, when the market house was built, which was probably in the sixteenth century, the whipping post was, in practice, one of its supporting pillars. Whipping was the standard punishment for petty theft and other minor offences and under the Poor Law of 1601 vagabonds were 'whipped on the bare back until bloody'. Whippings and public exposure in the stocks or pillory were usually reserved as a public spectacle on market days; but the whipping of women in public was abolished in 1830.

An Unusual Street Party

We think of our own times as given over to lawlessness, hooliganism and vandalism, so very unlike the good old days. In fact the disorders of today are trivial compared with what was once commonplace[5].

At Quarter Sessions at Devizes on 27 April 1731 a number of persons were indicted for riotous behaviour at Bradford on Avon when John Rogers, a scribbler (or wool carder), was in the stocks there for Sabbath-breaking[6].

On Monday 22 February 1731 churchwarden Richard Burcombe had brought Rogers before magistrate Thomas Methuen on a charge of tippling at the White Hart tavern during the hours of divine service on the previous day. Benjamin Cooper, who kept the White Hart, was likewise charged for permitting it. Both were convicted and Rogers was put in the stocks on the following Friday, 26 February. The stocks, being located at the market-house, only a few yards away from Cooper's pub, which stood at the corner of Silver Street and Market Street[7], were conveniently located for what followed, as a result of which Rogers, Cooper and others were remanded for trial on a charge of riotous assembly.

At the trial Richard Clare, goldsmith, stated in evidence that on Friday 26 February he was in the market place at Bradford when he saw John Rogers in the stocks in the Market House there, dressed in a long-tied wig, a very unusual dress for a scribbler.

He saw a female servant of Benjamin Cooper's bring a plate of meat and sauce from her master's house and put it on a stool near Rogers for him to eat while in the stocks. She also gave him a silver tankard of liquor to drink with it. The witness added that Rogers's sister continued to bring drink for him and for his friends gathered there.

It was clear that Rogers had many friends who disapproved of the action taken against him by Burcombe and Methuen. Among them were Benjamin Cooper, landlord of the White Hart, William Dicke, clothier, Joseph Dicke, baker, and Gabriel Cox, tallow chandler, who were calling to passers-by to come and join the party. A small boy, Edward Robert, was in the market place beating a drum and William Dicke called to him to come nearer and beat by the stocks, which he did.

At this the parish constable, clearly facing a situation which was already completely out of his control ordered the boy to stop beating there because it might give rise to a riot. Dicke called to the constable to leave the boy alone as he, Dicke, did not care how much noise he made. When Rogers was released from the stocks the boy, still beating his drum, accompanied him to the White Hart Inn.

Another witness, John Baker of Bradford, scribbler, said he was in the market place looking at people 'throwing at cocks' (for an explanation of this see Chapter 11 below) and saw Rogers in the stocks surrounded by his friends who were smoking and drinking out of a silver tankard and repeating the words 'maggot monger', referring, the witness believed, to Mr Burcombe, the churchwarden, wishing that he would come that way. The witness heard William Dicke say that it was not justice to put a fellow in the stocks for drinking a pint of ale and that a great many others deserved it more. A gentleman who was a stranger to the witness advised Dicke to say no more, to which Dicke replied that he did not care for anybody in the town and that stones and dirt were being thrown and one stone had hit him in the back.

Another witness, James Miles of Bradford, baker, stated that as he was riding through the market place when Rogers was in the stocks he saw a great many people there taking Rogers's part. William Dicke called out to him "Miles. Look here James, see what one of the pillars of the church has done out of malice". Another witness, John Newton of Bradford, said that William Dicke called out to passers by "This is the work of Burcombe who receives the Sacrament and then informs against a fellow out of malice".

Serious Unrest

There was good reason for confrontation and contempt for authority. The burst of prosperity of the last half of the previous century, had brought many newcomers seeking work. Now hard times were back. In 1726 unemployment and harsh national legislation gave rise to serious unrest. Under the new law, textile workers were forbidden to join 'combinations' or other clubs whose aims were the improvement of working conditions, better wages and a shorter working day. The penalty for joining such an organisation was imprisonment with hard labour.

There was, however, no law against employers forming themselves into committees to force on their workpeople onerous conditions, and some did so.

The ensuing riots alarmed the authorities and a company of soldiers (Colonel Churchill's Dragoons) was sent for and stationed in the town. Two weavers involved in a disturbance were, despite the advice of Trowbridge magistrate John Cooper, arrested on the orders of Bradford clothier magistrate, Thomas Methuen, and despatched to gaol at Salisbury with an escort of sixteen soldiers. The upshot was yet another riot, this time a really serious one. Called on to disperse, the rioters refused, whereupon the soldiers fired, killing one man and wounding two more.

John Cooper, clearly a sane and sympathetic soul, was now able to convince Methuen that he had been over-influenced by the hard-liners among the clothiers, particularly by a harsh and hated one called Heylyn, and had misjudged the situation. Methuen undertook to confer with Cooper in future.

We know all this from a letter which Cooper wrote to a Mr Earle in London for the attention of Lord Townshend.[8]

Unrest continued and the excellent Cooper was shortly to write to

London again, this time to the Home Secretary, the Duke of Newcastle, direct. He reported that some eight hundred weavers, 'armed only with sticks, being a parcel of half-starved wretches' were roving Bradford and rioting. Accompanied by a constable and thirty men he had spoken to some of them and listened to their complaints, which were that the clothiers were using weights of seventeen ounces to the pound and adopting other sharp practices by which, said the weavers, they were being obliged to weave four and five yards on every piece of cloth for nothing.

Cooper spoke to the clothiers who admitted the truth of this. The government, now greatly concerned, responded by sending a Mr Vaughan to investigate and report. Vaughan confirmed that the clothiers were to blame, in particular the oppressive and much hated Edward Heylyn.[9] Thereafter the unrest seems to have subsided for a while, more enlightened clothiers apparently having persuaded the others to behave better.

Priory Barn, formerly part of the Methuen estate, rescued from dereliction by Bradford on Avon Preservation Trust in the 1960s.

But throughout the eighteenth century riotous behaviour was endemic because so many were desperate and on the brink of starvation. The law was, nevertheless, implacable; a Bradford broadweaver who stole bacon in the course of a riot in 1766 was hanged for it. In 1787, as noted above, Belcombe Court was the scene of what might have developed into a serious riot.

There was trouble again in 1791. This time it was over the introduction of a scribbling machine by a clothier named Joseph Phelps, who lived at Westbury House, with a factory adjoining, in what is now the car park. On May 14 a mob of about five hundred assembled, demanding that Phelps should hand over the new machine or promise never to use it. Getting no response, the rioters began to hurl stones until all the windows in the house were broken and much of the furniture inside damaged. Phelps and his friends thereupon resorted to firearms. A man, a woman and a boy were killed and others wounded. But it only made matters worse. Phelps surrendered the machine. It was made of wood and the rioters dragged it to the bridge and set fire to it. In respect of the three dead the coroner's finding was 'justifiable homicide'. Phelps was awarded £250 compensation for damage to his property.

We have a graphic account of a serious riot one week-end in May 1826, thanks to a regimental history of the Wiltshire Yeomanry Cavalry[10]

On Saturday, 6th May, being market day at Bradford, the price of potatoes rose from 5d to 6d a peck. This circumstance caused great indignation among the lower orders, and a number of men set on an unfortunate market gardener, whom they accused of being the means of effecting the rise in price by forestalling the market. Having kicked and beaten him until he was left for dead, broken up his stall and divided his stock-in-trade, the mob proceeded to treat the other gardeners and greengrocers in a similar manner, and, having finished with them, went on to attack the butchers. The town was speedily filled with an immense disorderly crowd, and several well-known bad characters took the lead.

The special constables seized one of the ringleaders and locked him up (this will have been in the blindhouse on the bridge) only to have the mob rescue him by tearing off the roof. The rioting spread to Trowbridge where the mob wreaked havoc, among other things destroying the recently installed street gaslamps. Rioting continued all night in both towns until, in Bradford on Avon, a detachment of troops from Devizes arrived at daybreak on Sunday morning, to be followed soon after by detachments from Melksham, Warminster and Chippenham. Order was rapidly restored and the ringleaders were arrested and marched off to Fisherton gaol in the afternoon.

By the 1830s policing throughout the country was totally inadequate to deal with increasing lawlessness. Everywhere there was growing reluctance to travel at night, or unarmed, and there was concern at the lack of supervision of public houses and beer-shops.

Sir Robert Peel's London Metropolitan Force, formed in 1829, set the example of what was needed. In 1839 the Wiltshire authorities were first in the country to follow London's lead. They were spurred to do so by the fact that in May that year, amid the general unrest sparked by the Chartist movement, [11] they had had to borrow and station at Trowbridge a detachment of the London force. At Quarter Sessions at Marlborough on 15 October the magistrates agreed that the constables were the most inefficient and feeble men in the parish, both unable and unwilling to do any good. A committee meeting at Devizes on 31 October decided unanimously that a police force must be established in the county.

The force set up in Wiltshire had a Chief Constable (Captain Meredith RN), salary £400 a year, twelve superintendents (£75 a year) and 188 constables (seven shillings and sixpence a week plus great-coat, cape, frock coat and badge, two pairs of trousers, one pair of boots, one pair of shoes and a top hat). A constable could also have a small cutlass (a short sword, with a slightly curved blade) if needed for his personal protection in the performance of his duty, but it was only to be used at night or in sudden emergency.

At long last Bradford on Avon, like the rest of Wiltshire, was policed on a professional basis. The transformation from general lawlessness to order was dramatic. The police station was located at first at Bridge Foot, the north end of the town bridge. An old print shows that the stocks had then been moved to the other end of the bridge from their previous position by the old Market House. The blind-house on the bridge will have been found conveniently handy as guardhouse or lock-up. When the town hall building (now the Roman Catholic church) was erected in 1855 it inclu-ded a police station and cells and this part was duly occupied by an inspector and two constables who 'lived in'.

The new system placed emphasis on crime prevention: so a constable could arrest, for example, 'a drunken person or man in a violent passion who threatens the life of another' or in possession of housebreaking implements at night and suspected of the intent to burgle, or in possession of an offensive weapon. But he must not act hastily and must first watch closely the suspect to determine what he was about.

Everyone was happy until the rate bills came in and they found that the county rate had more than doubled by 1841 as a direct result of the cost of professional policing. There was a protest and many questioned whether the new force was value for money. In the end it was decided that it was, given that highway robbery had become rare and the crime of burglary had diminished.

From contemporary newspaper reports we know that the Bradford on Avon tradition of rowdiness continued, but that the police presence kept it well under control; in 1890, for example, the *Wiltshire Times* reported horseplay in the Shambles on Guy Fawkes night, with several hundred present, discharging squibs, crackers and pistols. With police officers living just across the road order was soon restored.

NOTES

1. Wiltshire Archaeological and Natural History Society Magazine volume 86 (1993), page 120.

2. In the words of William Langland's Piers Plowman he must

> *have an horne and be haywarde and liggen out a nyghtes*
> *And kepe my corn from pykers and theeves.*

By way of payment the hayward was allowed a piece of cornland adjoining the common pasture.

3. A hundred was originally the area deemed capable of supporting a hundred peasants and their households. The hundred of Bradford on Avon varied a little from time to time but mainly included the villages of Atworth, Broughton, Chalfield, Cumberwell, Monkton Farleigh, Trowle, Leigh, Woolley, Cumberwell, Holt, South Wraxall, Winsley and Limpley Stoke.

4. Under the Statute of Labourers of 1351 every township was required to provide and maintain stocks.
   The labour shortage brought about by the Black Death in 1348 had resulted in an unruly workforce, and up to three days in the stocks could be awarded for demanding wages higher than had been paid in 1348. Later on they became a form of summary punishment

for minor offenders, eg drunks (six hours), or for selling cigarettes on a Sunday (2 hours).

The Statute of Labourers was repealed in 1863 but did not expressly abolish the stocks and there are instances of their use after that, eg in the Butter Market at Newbury, Berks., on 11 June 1872. The stocks customarily stood in the most public location, either the village green or the market place. The punishment has still not been expressly abolished.

5. A specific aim in setting up in Bradford the free school for children of the poor was the 'encouragement of good manners' among them, an action reflecting the aims of the National Society for the Reformation of Manners formed about that time to combat drunkenness, swearing and public indecency.

6. From an article by B H Cunnington in the *Wiltshire Gazette* of 10 March 1932.
We know from court records of the day (for example eighteenth century magistrate William Hunt's Notebook published by the Wiltshire Record Society in 1981) that the Sabbath could be broken in a number of ways. The 'unlawful diversions', as they were called, seem to have included any kind of sport, for example climbing trees or shooting rooks, or buying and selling liquor during the hours of divine service. The standard penalty if the offender was an artisan or labouring man was three hours in the stocks, otherwise the penalty was a fine.

7. The White Hart was demolished in 1967 and the site is now an open space

8. Wiltshire Archaeological and Natural History Society cuttings book Vol 14 page 137.

9. Edward Heylyn was a Bradford clothier in a comparatively small way of business. He had premises in Bradford and also owned the watermill at Avoncliff. His business failed in 1737.(K Rogers – *Wiltshire and Somerset Woollen Mills.*)

10. 'The Annals of the Yeomanry Cavalry of Wiltshire by Henry Graham, being a complete history of the Prince of Wales' Own Royal Regiment from the time of its formation in 1794 to October 1884'.

11. The Chartist movement, intellectual left wing radical, but tinged with Methodism, did not, in the event, take Bradford on Avon by storm. Between mid 1838 and mid 1839 there were stirrings in the town and local groups were formed; but the excitement and apprehension generated elsewhere were absent.

The movement called for universal male suffrage, equal electoral districts, the ballot, annual parliaments and payment of members and no property qualification for them.

10.
RICH AND POOR

Poor relief

In medieval Bradford on Avon the landowners were the magnates; later on the clothiers were the rich ones. They were usually self-made men and classic capitalists. In the days of Edward III they were a privileged class, their livelihood virtually underwritten by royal decree, so much so that it was said later that in the clothing industry any dunce with money enough to deploy the wealth of skill readily available could quickly grow rich in it. The prudent among them (people like the Methuens, the Tugwells and the Yerburys) invested in property and, when the slump came, got out and did not come back. But many were the get-rich-quick parvenus who were tempted to live beyond their means, and, as the saying goes, went 'from clogs to clogs in three generations' – or even in one lifetime.

There were, as always, the chronically poor. From early times, and for many centuries, poor relief was seen as the business of the church. St Catherine's almshouses in Frome Road almost certainly had their origins in a medieval monastic foundation. There was also the hospital of St Margaret, usually thought of as a hospital for the leprous but possibly originally dedicated to poor relief.

After 1500, nationally, the gulf between rich and poor widened and the suppression of the monasteries, the traditional almsgivers, made, for the poorest, bad matters worse. Poverty became such that public order was seen to be under threat and the rest of the century saw a series of piecemeal counter-measures. At first these ranged from exhortations to the clergy to encourage greater Christian charity towards the truly needy, to, in the case of sturdy beggars, whipping, ear-cropping, branding on the shoulder, and even slavery.

Soon it became clear that central government must intervene in less drastic ways. From now on the parish was required to take financial responsibility; under the Poor Law of 1572 a parish rate must be levied by the vestry and 'overseers of the poor' appointed. It was probably about this time that what had been the leper hospital became the parish poorhouse. Later on there was to be another one, in Church Street. This one adjoined what is now called Dutch Barton cottage. (Afterwards the building became a brewery, since demolished). The century ended with the formulation of the Poor Law of 1601 which, amended and modified, continued to be for the local authorities their terms of reference for poor relief well into present century.

Exhortations to Christian benevolence did not fall on entirely deaf ears. In Bradford on Avon a number of charities, all linked with the parish church, survive to this day, their value greatly diminished. For example:

John Curll of Turleigh, by will dated 28 December 1703, left a farm and lands at Chirton for the benefit of the poor of Bradford and Freshford who lived by their honest labour. In Bradford on St Thomas's day 120 poor persons of Bradford and Winsley whom the vicar of Bradford should nominate were to have five shillings (25 pence) apiece and in Freshford 30 poor persons, whom the rector of Freshford should nominate were to have ten shillings.

Edward Thresher gave by will (exact date unknown but early 18th century) £100 to be distributed among the 'poor and impotent' people of Bradford and tything of Winsley who did not usually receive public alms of the parish. After 1823 the income of 50 shillings was used to buy shirts and shifts for the poor in Winsley only.

In 1951 the charity was benefiting about 71 persons, two shillings and sixpence in kind to each.

John Ferrett (1702-1770) gave by will £250 the income from which was to be used to purchase

for 20 poor men and women of the town of Bradford only, who do not receive alms of the parish, of sober and religious lives and conversation, and who constantly attend divine service in the parish church, when able, one sixpenny loaf each, to be delivered to them the first Sunday in the month, and at Christmas, Easter and Whitsuntide each year, immediately after morning service.

The same persons continued to receive the bread until their death. In 1951 the distribution was made annually in cash to about twenty-five persons.

Samuel Cam gave by will dated 29 June 1792 £100 to be distributed in bread to poor persons not receiving alms from the parish. The distribution was made at Christmas.

In 1951 about twenty-nine persons were entitled to three quarterns of bread each (a quartern was four pounds)

Mrs Elizabeth Tugwell, by her will dated 12 July 1799, gave £100, the income to be distributed yearly among 40 old infirm persons on 15th January.

In 1951 the distribution was one shilling and sixpence each (7 pence) to about forty persons.

John Strawbridge, by will dated 12 March 1805, gave £400 to the church-wardens of the parish of Bradford, the income from which was to be distributed yearly as crowns or half crowns as they should think proper to such poor persons of the parish as did not receive alms from the parish. The distribution was to be on St Thomas's day at the same time as the money from the Curll's Charity was given out. If possible recipients were to be different year by year.

In 1951 the distribution was half a crown (12 pence) to each of about sixty-seven persons.

Charlotte Amelia Beavan of Rochester, by her will dated 4 April 1873 gave £50, the income from it to be distributed to the poor in bread at the parish church of Bradford on Avon after divine service on Christmas Day each year.

In 1951 about twenty-five persons each received two quarterns of bread.

In the west wall of old Church House (Trinity Church hall) there is a narrow aperture, now blocked up. An old photograph shows it as it was in the last century; the photographer called it the dole window. So it was probably here that beneficiaries of the various charities in the town called for their dues *viz* bread or small amounts of money or whatever else was handed out on behalf of the trustees.

But this was no more than pious almsgiving of the kind that motivated John Hall to establish in 1700 the almshouse for four old men in what is now Frome Road. In his will Hall left £40 per annum for ever to keep the property in repair, to purchase gowns for the four inmates and to share out among them in weekly payments what was left. There were also the almshouses for poor old women (St Catherine's), described in Chapter 6 above[1]. But those on parish relief could not benefit from any of these charities. Such were often among those categorised as the 'undeserving' poor. Such charitable giving did nothing to tackle the underlying causes of poverty which resided in the attitude of *laissez faire* which prevailed until the nineteenth century. Nevertheless, until the eighteenth century, Bradford on Avon seems to have been a comparatively peaceful haven with no great problems of social disorder. But this was to change.

Degrees of exploitation of the weak, and abuse of power for private and personal gain are as old as the human race; but many Bradford on Avon clothiers were harsh beyond measure. It was extremely bad labour relations which led, in the eighteenth century, to the civil unrest described in Chapter 9, and which will have contributed to the eventual collapse of the whole West of England clothing industry. There was, quite literally, one law for the rich and another for the poor. The eighteenth century outlook is well illustrated by what happened to John Wesley's minister William Hitchens, who (see Chapter 4 above) was briefly incarcerated in the lock-up on the town bridge. The incident starkly reveals recruiting methods and social attitudes. The press-gang had seized what they took to be a propertyless itinerant stranger. The magistrates at first supported them. If a man had no property it was, to their way of thinking, quite appropriate that he should be sent to defend the property of those who had. When they found that Hitchens, too, was a property owner, he was immediately released.

The misery which assailed the Bradford on Avon underclass in the first half of the nineteenth century is touched upon in Chapter 3. Working-class people without resources other than such skills as they possessed lived permanently on the brink of destitution. Every penny that could be scraped together counted. Up to the end of the nineteenth century the family urine was a saleable commodity. The fullers used it – they called it sig – to remove the natural oil from raw wool,[2] and sent the sig-cart

Hall's Almshouses in Frome Road.

to make regular collections. All could earn a few coppers for the family by killing sparrows (a farthing paid by the vestry for each severed head), hedgehogs, otters, adders or martens at so much a corpse.

In 1834 there was new national legislation, deliberately framed to make life on parish relief so unpleasant that no-one would apply for it unless in the very direst need. For the next two decades, for many, life was grim indeed. Emigration to the colonies, encouraged and organised by the authorities, was a popular way out for those of working age.

The act (the Poor Law Amendment Act) provided for the creation of 'unions' of parishes, each with a workhouse administered by elected Boards of Guardians and centrally supervised by three Poor Law Commissioners appointed by central government. Bradford on Avon was designated the centre of a Poor Law union which comprised the parishes of Bradford, Broughton Gifford, Chalfield, Freshford, Monkton Farleigh, Westwood and Wingfield. Able-bodied persons seeking relief were forced to enter the workhouse where, as a discouragement to applications, conditions were made extremely hard. The 1834 legislation, with modifications, continued in force up to 1929.

The workhouse, newly founded in 1841, was at Avoncliff; in happier days the building had been a clothier's house and factory where work-people 'lived in'. The year 1841 was a disastrous one for Bradford's poor. It was the year the Hobhouse Bank in Church Street failed and many lost their savings. A number of small businesses failed and the workhouse, notwithstanding its terrors, was full.

The law required pauper husbands and wives to be accommodated separately. This was intended as an added hardship but was not always seen as such. In May 1888 the *Wiltshire Times* reported that at Avoncliff the inmates included a couple married over fifty years. The Guardians of the Poor, as they were called, in a benevolent mood furnished a room for their joint occupation, only to have it flatly rejected by both parties.

The plight of the workers

For those whose livelihood depended on what they could earn with their own hands, life had its ups and downs. For centuries Bradford on Avon had had a single industry based on the manufacture of clothing material. Heavily dependent on trade with the European mainland, it was vulnerable to forces it could not control, namely the machinations of king and central government. Skilled and semi-skilled labour, unorganised and therefore lacking political clout, was permanently at the bottom of the social heap and in times of recession came off worst.

The introduction of cost-cutting machinery towards the end of the eighteenth century was calamitous. As time went on wages were forced down and hours of work increased. In 1785 wages in Frome, a rival woollen town, were

weaver	20 shillings a week
female hand	8 shillings a week
child worker 7-8 yrs 'for attending the machines'	2 shillings and sixpence a week
labourer	16 to 18 pence a day

A working week was six days.
Typical prices were:

Beef and mutton	5 pence a pound
veal	6 pence a pound
butter	11 pence a pound
bread	13 pence a pound

The figures speak for themselves. To buy bread and butter for two days (say a two pound loaf and half a pound of butter) a labourer must work two whole days of twelve hours. Small wonder that there should be general discontent.

Child and female labour was exploited to the limit.

Between 1815 and 1846 the Corn Laws, which kept the price of grain artificially high in the interest of the landowners, brought even greater hardship.

Men of conscience sought to remedy matters. We know that rich Bradford on Avon clothier Ezekiel Edmonds campaigned for the abolition of the Corn Laws. Up in Lancashire rich mill-owner, philanthropic Robert Owen, in 1819 introduced legislation which forbade the employment of children under the age of nine. Although this particular legislation did not work because the magistrates were the mill-owners, or the friends of mill-owners, and it went largely disregarded and unenforced, it led to Lord Shaftesbury's Factory Act of 1832. In future there were to be limits on the extent that children were employed in textile mills and inspectors were appointed to enforce these limits. Children between the ages of nine and thirteen were to work not more than nine hours a day and those between thirteen and eighteen not more than twelve hours. From 1844 the maximum for women was twelve hours a day, from 1853 it was ten and a half hours and the same for all workers under eighteen. From 1874 the working day for women was reduced to ten hours and children under ten were not to be employed at all.

Right up to the present century the existence of a pawnshop in the town speaks of the financial straits in which some of the poorest regularly found themselves and the occasional local press item[3] throws a shaft of light on the social scene. In 1890 Ellen Ottridge of Wine Street found herself in court. Pawnbroker Mrs. Taylor of Church Street advanced one and sixpence halfpenny (eight pence today) on a woollen skirt, the real value of which she estimated to be three shillings and sixpence (seventeen pence). But the skirt had, alas, been stolen by Mrs Ottridge who had needed money to buy food for her children. Lifelong Bradfordian Jim King tells me that there was real hunger in the early years of the present century and there was a soup kitchen in Barton Orchard run by Mrs. Beddoe of Chantry House.

The Better-off

In the eighteenth and nineteenth centuries the gap between the few very rich and the many very poor was wider than ever. Midway between them there were those professional people, tradesmen and skilled artisans who were comfortably off, and for them Bradford on Avon was a very pleasant place to live. Listed in the *Universal British Directories* of the late eighteenth century under the heading 'principal inhabitants', we find that the town could then sustain two lawyers, three medical practitioners, five grocers, five bakers, four shoemakers, three butchers, three linen-drapers, three tailors, three clockmakers, three carpenters, two coopers, a tallow-chandler, a tanner, a maltster, a glover, a milliner and a chinaware shop. There were seventeen clothiers, one of them, John Renison, a grocer and postmaster as well.

A little surprisingly (for Bradford on Avon) we learn that there was evidently work enough for two peruke makers, a high-fashion trade one might suppose more appropriate in contemporary Bath. But Humphrey Tugwell is wearing a peruke in Gainsborough's portrait of him, see

Chapter 6 above; so perhaps it was the thing in Bradford on Avon too. Of the three medical practitioners, Walter Brown was a surgeon, while Mr Bethell and Robert Cooper practised as surgeon and man-midwife. The two lawyers were Joseph Smith and Daniel Clutterbuck, the latter also listed as a banker. Also named were William Bush, schoolmaster, and the parish clerk, John Nibley.

Edward Hopkins, Joseph Moxon and James Moxon were clockmakers. Earlier in the century there had been the Rudd family, Joshua, who made fine clocks, some of them still going in Bradford on Avon today, and his son Edward, who in 1784 was paid two guineas for repairing the church clock.

NOTES

1. We know from the report of an enquiry held on behalf of the Charity Commissioners on 13 February 1901 that those in Hall's Almshouses were rather better off than those in St Catherine's, clearly because of the scandalous misappropriation in the past of the latter's endowment.

In 1834 three almswomen in St Catherine's were entitled to two shillings and sixpence a week when funds were available. From 1861, when the Charity Commissioners intervened, this was increased to four shillings a week. They were also given five hundred-weight of coal at Christmas by a local coal company. The minimum age was sixty and married couples were not allowed.

The men in Hall's Almshouse were allowed to have their wives with them. In 1834 they were being given three shillings and sixpence a week plus a pair of shoes every year and a coat every second year. In 1901 the weekly allowance was five shillings and they were being allowed two coats a year, one for the summer and one for the winter. In 1908 the weekly allowance was 7s 6d. In 1960 the weekly allowance ceased and in 1963 a weekly rent of ten shillings was introduced.

2. See *Wiltshire and Somerset Woollen Mills* by Kenneth Rogers, published in 1976. In Trowbridge Mr Rogers's father recalled the weekly round of the sig-cart and the emptying of the earthenware jars left at many houses.

3. *Wiltshire Times* 30 August 1890.

11.
LIFE STYLE

PUBS, CLUBS AND GOING TO CHURCH

Inns, taverns and beerhouses.

In towns and counties to the west they drank cider, but in Bradford on Avon it was beer. It is possible that Bradfordians were brewing and drinking beer in the Iron Age. It is almost certain that they were, like their contemporaries elsewhere in Britain, brewing and drinking it in Roman times. The Roman historian Tacitus, writing in about AD 97, drew attention to 'a wine made from barley' in Britain. From the early Middle Ages social life centred on beer-drinking, which took place in local pub and parish church alike.

In the Middle Ages the typical brewer and vendor of beer was female – an ale-wife – and she kept the ale-house, distinguishable by its ale-stake and bush of leaves. Beer has remained paramount, even with the introduction of cheap gin in the eighteenth century. Throughout the nineteenth century there were never fewer than twenty licensed houses in the town and after 1830 there were ten beerhouses as well. Pubs were blamed for drunkenness and fighting and, by way of antidote, the British and Foreign Temperance Society established a temperance hall in Sladesbrook and a temperance hotel in the town centre. But 'drunk and disorderly' is not a modern offence; national laws for the conduct of pubs go back to at least 1375.

Inns, furnishing social intercourse on a higher level than pubs and alehouses, had beds for travellers and served wider social needs, such as formal meetings; by the nineteenth century, before the town hall (now the Roman Catholic church) was built in 1855, the town authorities would meet at the Swan. Contemporary directories record that in the eighteenth century the New Bear (now Silver Street House) was the town's other principal inn. Not nearly so fashionable, but an important centre of

Silver Street House was renovated by Bradford on Avon Preservation Trust in 1977. Left: the building before rehabilitation, right: as it is now.

Methodism, was the Maidenhead Inn in Market Street, (now the Town Club), dating back to the seventeenth century and run in John Wesley's day by the redoubtable Methodist Richard Pearce. Until 1818, when a new Methodist chapel was built on Coppice Hill, it was both inn and Methodist centre. Pearce owned also the Cross Keys Inn in St. Margaret Street (now Frome Road) which, like the Maidenhead, furnished both social life and spiritual uplift.[1]

In Woolley the Crown Inn appears first in the records in 1848. By 1879 the George was there too.

Social Life: Church and Chapel

The parish church was by tradition, from the earliest times on, the centre of a town's social life for all classes. With the growth of nonconformity in the town the chapel congregations were equally centres of social life. To judge by the number of prosperous clothiers whose names appear together in connexion with the chapels they were doubtless also useful centres for business contacts and arrangements.

Every parish had its church house for meetings and socials. In Bradford on Avon it was the building in Church Street called now Trinity Church Hall. Here it was that fund-raising church-ales were held, jolly boozy occasions customarily held at Easter and Whitsun and other holidays and festivals whenever extra money was needed for repairs and maintenance at the church. The beverage was a strong ale of good quality, specially brewed for the occasion from malt traditionally provided by the church-wardens and stored at the church house till the great day. In Bradford on Avon the storage area was the cross-wing of the building. Church-ales go back to the early 1200s.

Before Church House was built by Thomas Horton in the early 1500s the spacious nave of the church itself will have been used for social gatherings. In a borough as rich and important as Bradford on Avon then was, the congregation will have enjoyed organ music from very early on, perhaps from soon after the church was built.

Organs began early in Wiltshire. Malmesbury Abbey had one in the eighth century (Aldhelm's time) and Salisbury Cathedral had one in the tenth century. By the thirteenth century they were common in the larger parish churches and by the end of the Middle Ages almost general, only to be removed in Oliver Cromwell's time.

At the Restoration organs were reintroduced into cathdrals and larger churches; but until the nineteenth century most parish churches made do with an orchestra, or, from the eighteenth century, a barrel-organ.

In Bradford on Avon the vestry installed a new organ in 1729. It was a good one and much prized; money spent on it for maintenance and for paying the organist and organ-blower was not begrudged. In 1784 when it was showing signs of wear, Henry Coster of Salisbury, organ builder, was paid £40 for repairs. Thirteen years later more repairs were needed and one Maddey was paid £162 for them. At the same time the vestry authorised the payment of substantial sums for gilding the case and for the purchase of blue cloth, blue fringe and lace to make curtains to the organ gallery. It was clearly a showpiece and the *Universal British Directory* for 1793 noted it as one of the town's attractions.

Merry England took a knock under Cromwell's Commonwealth; church-ales ceased and church organs were destroyed. Church-ales were never resumed. By this time nonconformity and dissent were widespread, and by the end of the eighteenth century were so strong that the parish church took second place in social life. This trend was to continue. When Canon Jones arrived on the scene in 1851 the parish church building was so neglected that he was dismayed. His immediate predecessors, Henry Harvey (1835-1850) and Frederic William Blomberg seem to have done nothing in the way of maintenance. In a talk to a group of fellow-clerics which he gave at Clevedon on 15 October 1885, only a few days before his sudden death, he described what he found:

My first visit was paid in the month of November, 1850, on a dull and foggy day. My heart sank within me when I first saw the church. It had galleries on the east, the north and the west. In the centre of the south nave was a pew allotted to the vicar. Next to it, on the west side, was a long pew in which sat six old women looking eastward, and on the east side a still larger pew, which held eight old men, looking westward. My wife soon petitioned me to get some other seat allotted to her less exposed to public gaze. Above the vicar's pew rose 'Pelion, Ossa and Olympus' in the desk and pulpit arrangements. The pews were of all shapes and sizes, and in all manner of position...

We were lighted by simple dips, which of a winter evening just made darkness visible. The noise made by creaking old snuffers was at times distracting; the poorer folk used a simpler apparatus for snuffing the dips.

By this time the organ had been abandoned. The canon continued:-

In 1851 our choir sat in a western gallery and was led by diverse instruments, flute, fiddle, violoncello and on special occasions we had a french horn and a trombone.

The building itself was in very poor shape, the walls out of perpendicular, the arches and columns in such a state as to render it unsafe, the roof in disrepair. Not without opposition (the numerous and influential nonconformists objected to any levy on church rate) Canon Jones succeeded in raising funds for a complete restoration of the fabric of the building and refurbishment of the interior. The cost of between £4,000 and £5,000 was defrayed entirely by public subscription. The work completed – it took two years – the church was re-opened with great local acclaim on 13 February 1866.

Leisure activities: self-improvement
The educational developments and the extension of the franchise during the nineteenth century gradually brought about social change. By now the Trinity Church National School and the British School had been going for some time and a good many Bradfordians in all walks of life could manage the three Rs. In 1839 there was a public circulating library with 295 subscribers, the charge being twopence a volume. From *The Dorset and Wiltshire Directory* for 1865 we learn of 'a reading room for working men opened in 1863 under the auspices of the clergy'. We are told that there was 'a large number of subscribers amongst the class for whose benefit it was founded and more particularly intended.' It was 'well frequented'. Daily and weekly newspapers and magazines were on the tables, and there was a good library for the use of the members.

For the moneyed and truly literate there was the Literary Institution, adjoining the town hall (now the Roman Catholic Church of St Thomas More) which was open daily from eight o'clock in the morning to ten at night and where lectures were delivered during the winter season. Membership was by subscripion: £1 annually or £10 for life. The fee for ladies was 7s.6d per annum.

The political parties of the day were represented by the Liberal Club in St Margaret's Street and the Conservative Club at 21 Church Street. The rooms of both were open daily from eight in the morning to ten at night. Each had daily and weekly newspapers and magazines on the tables and both offered a billiard table, chess, drafts and other board games for the use of members. Subscription at each was one shilling per quarter.

Ancient customs

Ancient customs, usually rooted in religious observance, whether pagan or Christian, regulated the rhythm of the year.

It is quite likely that the 'Cattern cakes' customarily eaten in Bradford on St Catharine's Day (25 November) right up Canon Jones's time dated back, like hot cross buns, (which derive from the medieval practice of giving consecrated bread marked with a cross on Good Friday) to medieval times and were connected with the chapel dedicated to St Catherine, which tradition says stood where St Catherine's Almshouses now stand.

Canon Jones, writing in 1859, stated

> It may be mentioned ...that there is still the remnant of the observance of a holiday on St Catherine's Day. Within a few years only, cakes called cattern cakes were made in considerable numbers and sent by the bakers to their customers, Many of the old people reckon their ages by the festival of this Saint. A very short time ago an old bed-ridden woman said to the writer of this paper in true Wiltshire, and, we may add, very fair Anglo-Saxon – (and really they are often convertible terms), – "I'll be vower-score come Kattern-tide, and I beant yeable now to doff or don myself" which, in modern English meant, "I shall be four-score next St Catherine's-tide, and I am not able now to undress (do-off) or dress (do-on) myself".

Another link with the saint whom Bradford folk possibly thought of as their patron may be the decorative symbol which appears in the east wall of the chancel of Holy Trinity Church, a small circle enclosing a cross suggesting the four spokes of a wheel.

Every Spring, well into the last century, they 'clipped the church'. The ceremony will have been an ancient pagan one, adopted, like many others, by the Christian church, The centrality of a moving circle to the performance of this particular one suggests that it was originally a tribute to the sun derived from its apparent circular movement across the sky to the underworld. Its latter-day purpose seems to have been to protect the building from the activities of the devil for the ensuing year.

In his history of the town, Canon Jones describes it. Until the churchyard was enclosed, on the morning of Shrove Tuesday, from time immenorial, a bell had been tolled. Shortly after the bell ceased, all the apprentices and schoolboys of the town clustered in great numbers in the churchyard and sought by joining hands, entirely to encircle the church. When the circle was complete, there was much jumping and shouting.

A letter in a local newspaper (*The Advertiser*) in 1881 shows that the custom lingered for a while in a modified form. J Hanny, a former resident in the town, wrote that when he was a schoolboy (presumably a little before Canon Jones's time) children would, at by about seven or eight o'clock in the evening, gather in the churchyard to join hands and walk round the church three times. (With numbers too few to make the symbolic circle they clearly invoked the magic of three and substituted a triple perambulation.) Daniel Batchelor also remembered it from the early days of the century.

The rite was observed elsewhere in slightly different particulars. In the parish church at Rode there hangs a picture painted by W.W.Wheatley on Shrove Tuesday night 1848 which shows the men of the village holding hands to encircle the church and dancing around it. It seems that the custom continues (or has been revived) at Painswick in Gloucestershire.[1]

Another Shrove Tuesday custom was the barbaric 'flinging at cocks', described below.

There were odd customs and rituals peculiar to the parish church. Canon Jones told how when he first arrived in Bradford on Avon at the beginning of January 1851

> The Christmas 'decorations' were still remaining. They consisted simply of small twigs of laurel or laurastinus stuck into holes made by a large gimlet at the top of the pews. They called it 'sticking the church'
>
> Some queer old customs remained. At the saying of each 'Gloria' the men bowed and the women curtseyed; and many of them who sat looking westward turned to the east. We had one very absurd custom. After a funeral, when what were called 'fittings' were allowed, a hat, duly arrayed, was hung the next Sunday on a peg behind the pulpit. The clerk, who also held the office of sexton, often had two hat-bands given to him; and the two hats were were duly suspended behind his desk. There was no little flutter of excitement when I ventured to discountenance this custom.

Up to at least the middle of the nineteenth century curfew (first instituted under King Alfred the Great as a fire precaution during the hours of darkness and fixed under William the Conqueror at eight o'clock) was still being rung every evening and morning in the winter months. Vestry records show that the sexton was paid £5 a year for ringing it; payment included keeping the clock wound and setting the chimes.

Mayday which, also, had pagan origins, was celebrated nation-wide. From at least the Middle Ages till the end of the eighteenth century it was a major public holiday with great festivities and we may be sure that in Bradford on Avon, as everywhere else, it was the custom for girls and boys to get up at dawn and go a-maying to fetch branches of trees and flowers to decorate houses and streets and that there will have been morris-dancing, dancing around the maypole and a Queen of the May.

Daniel Batchelor recalled that in the 1830s, when he was a small boy, 'the jolly wassailers with their loud songs and expectant punch bowl' toured the town at Christmas time. The custom was for young women to go from door to door offering a drink of spiced ale and expecting a small gratuity in return. (*Wes hal* was a Saxon greeting – 'good health'). He also recalled 'noisy skimmertons'.[2]

Sports and pastimes.

We may be sure that the sports, games and other pastimes beloved of our ancestors were as much pursued in Bradford on Avon as anywhere else in England. Most of these were simple and called for physical exertion. Typical would be morris-dancing, vaulting, pitching the bar, backswords, archery, church-bell ringing, darts, bowling, football (once discouraged because it frequently led to violence), wrestling, cricket, stool-ball (a variation of cricket usually played by ladies, occasionally joined by men) and so on. Quieter and a little less innocent, being played for gain, were pitch and hustle (played with halfpennies), five-stones and throwing dice, the churchyard being a popular meeting-place for engaging in the last two. At fairs there will have been sack-races, wheelbarrow races, jingling matches (a kind of blind man's buff played with hand-bells) and hunting the pig (catching the animal by its tail, which had been well-soaped.) Least attractive of all were the spectacle of bull-baiting and the 'sport' of cock-throwing, or flinging at cocks.

We know where in the town they practised archery and played tennis and where they watched bull-baiting and took part in cock-throwing.

Hang-dog Alley led from Church Street to the bull-pit.

The butts for practising archery were near the parish church. The inquest on George Cuthbert of Bradford, mercer, reveals that he was accidentally killed during target practice there in June 1573, being struck on the head by an arrow launched by his friend Robert Fyppe, also of Bradford, tailor.

Although in the sixteenth century the long bow was still officially a weapon of war, in Bradford on Avon archery by this time will have been no more than a pastime.

The churchyard, and in particular the wall of the tower, was the place for tennis. Canon Jones commented in his history of the town that the south wall of the church tower showed unmistakeable evidences of having been used for the balls of the tennis players.

The street called Bull Pit, near the Swan Hotel, reminds us of the spectacle of bull-baiting, popular in England from at least the Middle Ages. The bull was tied by the horns with a rope about fifteen feet long which was fixed to a stake driven into the ground. Trained dogs were let loose in turn. The object was to 'pin the bull' – success came when the dog seized the bull by the nose and held on.

Bull-baiting frequently gave rise to public disorder, and largely because of this was made illegal in 1835. It had ceased in Bradford on Avon long before that.

At a trial in 1731 (see Chapter 9), a witness mentioned that he had been watching the 'flinging at cocks' in Bradford market place. Flinging at cocks was an old English custom, traditionally practised on, but not confined to, Shrove Tuesday, which dated back at least to the days of Geoffrey Chaucer. Lengths of wood called cock-steles were hurled at a tied cock, the bird being won by whoever knocked it down and caught it before it got up again. A variant was to assail it till it was killed.[3]

Backswords was a form of sport similar to fencing, played with wooden cudgels called backswords or jostling sticks. The object was to strike your opponent on the forehead and draw blood. Some years ago a pair of these was found in the attic of 10 Mason's Lane when it was the British Legion Club.

Church bell ringing, though very much a recreational activity, had a wider significance. The English love of strenuous exercise and of such loud noises as the firing of cannon, beating of drums and the ringing of bells, noted by sixteenth century German traveller Hentzner,[4] was deployed by the vestry who, as the records show, were always ready to spend money on bell-maintenance. Bells offered something to everyone. They celebrated royal occasions and famous victories. They brought to remote Bradford on Avon news of happenings in a world beyond the woollen mill and the market place of which hitherto many parishioners were only vaguely aware. Tidings of glamorous victories on land or sea lent point to the blandishments of the recruiting sergeant and the depredations of the press gang. And ringing the bells was such fun. There was exercise, gallons of beer and, in days before the electronic amplifier, the opportunity to raise a din, all with the approval of the powers that be. In 1885 Daniel Batchelor recalled a great occasion in which his father took part on 7 September 1799. This was the ringing of Holts Grandsire, when there were 5040 changes in three hours and twenty five minutes, the ringers each with an attendant who plied him with bread soaked in brandy. The ringing only ended when one William Gibbs, on the heavy seventh, fell exhausted to the floor. (The feat is recorded on a mural tablet in the tower.)

The Bradford Rifle Volunteers

Playing at soldiers has been popular, with some Englishmen, from the days of the militia and train-bands to Dad's Army and the Sealed Knot; and poking fun at their activities has long been the pastime of other Englishmen.

At the time of the Napoleonic Wars, when it appeared that England might be under threat of invasion, Bradford citizens formed an 'armed Association for the defence of the Hundred of Bradford'. At the inaugural meeting at the Swan Hotel on April 30 1798 it was decided to form two companies of fifty men each.

With the defeat of Napoleon at Waterloo the threat passed, but in the 1850s Louis Napoleon (Napoleon III) was making threatening noises and it looked as if the country might again be under threat. Though, in the event, it was Austria that was attacked, nevertheless Ezekiel Edmonds, leading clothier and a Justice of the Peace, and other important Bradfordians, managed to convince themselves, as rival towns had done, that invasion by the French was imminent and that rifle volunteers must be called for.

On 19 December 1859 they convened a public meeting, and decided to go ahead with recruitment. Edmonds was elected chairman unanimously. Subscription lists were opened, with a special one 'for the ladies'. (The ladies were to prove most generous, particularly when money for uniforms was appealed for.) In the event the scheme was to give a splendid boost to social activities in the town, with fund-raising bazaars and celebratory dinners at the Swan.

By the next meeting, twelve days later, enough names had been enrolled to form a company. Ezekiel Edmonds was appointed commanding officer, with Captain Pickwick and Mr Forster of Holt as subalterns. But Captain Pickwick, a retired regular soldier, refused to serve under a civilian, so Ezekiel Edmonds stood down and Pickwick replaced him. Dr William Adye was appointed honorary assistant surgeon and Canon Jones, the vicar, was appointed chaplain. Applegate and George Adye, William's brother, were appointed sergeants.

In *The 1st Battalion Wilts Volunteers 1861-1885*, published by W H Allen in 1888, Major Robert Dwarris Gibney, Indian Army (rtd), gives a somewhat tongue-in-cheek account of it all.

The first drill was on 24 January 1860 at Spackman's dye-house (now St Margaret's Hall). As Major Gibney put it:-

> ...as every man thought it necessary to come armed with a gun of some sort, and also as with this gun (perhaps an old flint musket of the Georges' time, or a flimsy single-barrel sparrow-killer) he was to go through the manoeuvres and platoon, and appear in the ranks generally, the teaching of musketry must have been utter foolery, and the movements of our Bradford volunteers somewhat ludicrous. However, these like other volunteers survived the ridicule, and notwithstanding Punch's 'Who shot the dog?' and the wondrous wit displayed by street boys or by those disliking the movement, but whose position and education should have taught them better, drilled steadily on...

A rifle range was established in what we now call the Country Park. Major Gibney continued:-

> The ground selected as a practice ground was an easy one to shoot over, the steep turfy hill against which the targets were placed forming an excellent background; but by whom the said range was passed as a rifle range deponent sayeth not. He could not have been to Hythe, or had much notion of the erratic flight of an elongated projectile, or of the difficulty even the best-drilled soldiers in the service find in avoiding accidents,

where your line of fire extends across sundry footpaths, a canal, and a railroad. That there were no accidents is attributable more to good luck than good guidance. The shorter ranges across the canal were tolerably secure. A red flag, much shouting and an occasional despatch of one of the squad to the dangerous point managed to stay man, woman or child from running into danger and informed the cursing bargee of his being cared for; but when it came to long distances, where shouts and signals were unheeded, or where the height of the trajectory was deemed safety sufficient, then came a question as to whom was the sanction of this being used as a range due.

The Great Western Railway Company evidently for very many years troubled themselves not about such trifles as bullets through their carriages...

The uniform selected by the Bradford Corps was an excellent one – of course fitting the body too tightly; but this screwing in of a man's waist and throttling him with a stock was considered the proper thing to do, and even has a value in some elderly gentleman's view of the smart soldier...

By November 1861 they had been joined with Trowbridge and Westbury to form a battalion. Battalion parades were, however, ragged, as the companies tended to turn up at various times and to depart suddenly before the end to catch the last train home.

In 1867, according to the *Post Office Directory of Dorsetshire, Wiltshire and Hampshire* the 9th Wilts Volunteers, as they were now called, numbered about sixty efficient members.

In 1893 they were called E Company, 1st Wilts Rifle Volunteers. Their commanding officer was Captain Thomas Herbert Clark and the Lieutenants were John A Adye, H A Adye and J Compton. (John Compton was headmaster of the County School later re-named Fitzmaurice Grammar School). Their armoury was at The Stores, Silver Street. According to the Bradford on Avon Annual of that year their target practice ground was still the Country Park, 'near the Swing Bridge on the canal'.

From *Kelly's Directory* 1907 we know that they were still called E Company) and that a cyclist company of a hundred efficient members had been added. The company was swallowed up by the First World War, never to be revived.

NOTES

1. The Cross Keys Inn was pulled down to make way for the railroad. It was one Bradford on Avon pub where moderation prevailed; Pearce is said never to have allowed a customer to have more than a pint of beer at a time. In his study entitled *Class Meetings in relation to the Design and Success of Methodism* (1873) the Reverend S W Christophers recounted that an elderly lady of his acquaintance told him that, in 'one happy pilgrim's home', (as she called Pearce's pub) there was a little whitewashed room behind the bar, set aside for Methodist meetings which were never interrupted by anything from without. It was to her a holy place.

2. *A Guide to the Traditional Customs of Britain*, published in 1985 by The National Trust.

3. Skimmington or skimmenton-riding, defined in *Wiltshire Words*, (first published in 1894 and re-published by the Wiltshire Life Society in 1991), as:

> A serenade of rough music got up to express disapproval in cases of great scandal and immorality. The orthodox procedure in North Wilts is as follows: the party assembles before the houses of the offenders, armed with tin pots and pans, and performs a serenade for three successive nights. Then after an interval of three nights the serenade is repeated for three more. Then another interval of the same duration and a third repetition of the rough music for three nights – nine nights in all. On the last night the effigies of the offenders are burnt.

4. Literary references to the custom are numerous. Samuel Pepys wrote in his diary on Shrove Tuesday 26 February 1661:-

> Very merry, and the best fritters that ever I eat in my life. After that looked out at window; saw the flinging at cocks.

Sir Thomas More (1477-1535) wrote with pride of his skill, as a young man, at casting the cock-stele.

5. ' ...so that it is common for a number of them that have got a glass in their heads to get up into some belfry and ring the bells for hours together for the sake of exercise.' Hentzner, quoted by Joseph Strutt in his *Sports and Pastimes of the People of England* (1801 edition).

Above: Market Street winding downhill towards the Town Bridge. Pippett Buildings, restored by Bradford on Avon Preservation Trust in 1982, on the right; Swan Hotel in distance. Below: The Shambles

12.
GOING SHOPPING

Markets and market day.

Bradfordians have made their day-to-day purchases in the Shambles for the past thousand years or so. The name is derived from the Anglo-Saxon word *scamel*, meaning a small bench or stool on which goods were exposed for sale. The goods displayed were usually meat and a shambles came to be in effect, a meat market. The word came to mean also a slaughter-house – which was what the meat market was anyway. Adjacent to the Shambles at the east end was the earliest market house and on the south side (the lower end of Silver Street) was the market place. There were no shops in the modern meaning of the word, though there were workshops from which the product manufactured might sometimes be bought.

We can be pretty sure that Bradford's Shambles and market began in Saxon times. But after the Norman Conquest all market rights became vested in the king, who, in Bradford's case, delegated them exclusively to the lord of the manor who, in those days, happened to be the abbess of Shaftesbury. At the Domesday survey in 1086 the market was valued at 45 shillings.

From before Norman times right up to the beginning of the present century Bradford was an important market town to which farmers and other folk came from miles around to buy and sell. On market days (Monday and Saturday in 1793 according to local directories and Saturday in 1867 'except for corn, cattle and cheese' when it was every other Tuesday) the market place will have been crowded with livestock and stalls laid out with produce. In the parapet of the town bridge there are small rings which were used to tether beasts awaiting sale, (and no doubt also served to tether the bull awaiting torment at the nearby bull-baiting pit).

The exclusive right to hold a market or a fair was a valuable source of regular income for the lord of the manor. Only he could grant a pitch and each stall-holder had to pay what he demanded.[1] To ensure that produce was not intercepted, and sold on the way to market, and the lord of the manor thus deprived of his dues, it was made an offence, punishable in the manorial court, to 'forestall' – to buy or sell before the goods actually got on to the market stall. It was equally in the lord's interest that the market should be well-run, with cheating kept to a minimum. He therefore appointed coroners of the market whose duties were to check weights and measures and to ensure fair dealing generally. The coroner of the market was authorised to settle disputes on the spot under *piedpoudre* procedure (see Chapter 6, note 7).

In the sixteenth century it became the practice in England to erect market halls, often a pillared space where traders had stalls, with a room above to serve as the town hall. A building of that kind once stood at the foot of Coppice Hill, at the east end of the Shambles. As was customary, stocks and whipping post were set up there, too.

Bradford market rights belonged to the lord of the manor until 1882, when Sir Charles Hobhouse, Bt, sold them to the Town Commissioners for £250.

Fairs

Fairs were much bigger events than markets and sometimes went on for more than one day. As with markets, the right to hold them was the prerogative of the lord of the manor. They were major events in the commercial life of any town, and from records of church and other committee meetings we know that they were given over-riding priority; the fair came first – a committee could wait. Bradford Trinity fair was held on Trinity Monday (in June). It stretched along Church Street and according to Canon Jones's history 'the booths at the time of the annual fair on Trinity Monday were in olden times brought close to the limits'. This was the day when farm labour was hired for the ensuing year. In Daniel Batchelor's day the cattle and horse fairs extended from Timbrells in St Margaret's Street(now the car park) up to the old poorhouse beyond the Cross Keys Inn (both pub and poorhouse were demolished in 1846 to make way for the railway station).

From at least 1756 up to the early years of the present century another fair was held on the common at Bradford Leigh on the first Monday after St Bartholomew's Day (24 August).

Fairs were frequently the occasion for fights, hooliganism and general disorder with pitched battles between gangs of louts from neighbouring towns and villages. There were, in particular, regular set-tos between gangs calling themselves respectively Bradford Gudgens and Trowbridge Nobs. Daniel Batchelor remembered Dan Holiday's annual visit to Trowbridge fair to 'wollop the Knobs'. Readers familiar with *Kilvert's Diary* will recall similar regular battles between Chippenham and Langley.

In Bradford, fairs in the old-fashioned sense were discontinued altogether in the early years of the present century. The street market in the old market place ceased to be held about the same time.

NOTE

1. It may be noted that such valuable ancient rights survive to this day. An item in *The Times* Newspaper of 13 November 1989 reported that the right to hold the market at Newmarket in Suffolk had changed hands. The 'new market' (which gave the town its name) began in 1257 under a charter of Henry III. This conferred the right to hold a market and to exclude any other within a league (three miles) of the town. Since 1920 the owners had been the Jockey Club, who up to 1989 leased it to the town for £150 a year. On recent renewal of the lease they asked £24,000 a year but had compromised by selling to the town for £300,000.

13.
TRAVEL, TRANSPORT AND KEEPING IN TOUCH

Until the eighteenth century the British were not road-conscious. The Romans, militaristic and highly organised, had had their own good reasons for building excellent roads and maintaining communications. Celts and Saxons saw no such need; when they went anywhere they went on foot or used the river.

So, for long centuries, towns like Bradford on Avon remained relatively isolated. Communications were local and roads little more than tracks. Such ways as there were evolved because of circumstances. When Aethelred's guilty conscience prompted him, in 1001, to make over the manor of Bradford to the abbess of Shaftesbury he chose it for its remoteness. Thereafter it will have become less remote, with regular intercourse between the abbey and the manor; so the folk memory of a track leading from Shaftesbury over Salisbury Plain, later crossing the river at Barton Bridge, and what is now the railway line, to Bath, Bristol and the sea, is likely to be well-based. Barton Bridge, pack-horse width and without parapets, could accommodate wide loads of farm produce or anything else.

Indifferent repairs and maintenance meant dust-ridden ways in summer, quagmires in winter. Long-distance travel was uncomfortable and dangerous. For centuries, roads were a parish responsibility, with residents required by statute to provide six days' unpaid labour every year, using their own implements and carts. The job was invariably done badly, usually amounting to no more than filling holes. The 'surveyor' appointed by the vestry to supervise the work and see that it was carried out by midsummer was customarily appointed for his general standing and authority in the town rather than for his knowledge or experience of road repair. In 1749 we find, for example, Francis Yerbury, rich clothier and inventor of cassimere, holding the office. But though passengers shied off, goods got through. From 1740 there were weekly runs from London and these increased as time went on and road surfaces improved. From 1752 a succession of road acts set out to improve matters for passengers. But Bradford on Avon was never on the main London to Bath route and so remained largely unaffected by the rudimentary system of public transport by stage coach which developed on the Great West Road. From 1777 there was a turnpike to Box, to join it there for journeys to the capital, and from 1792 the present Bath Road was built; but for most Bradfordians it was still rarely more than local journeys on horseback, by horse-drawn waggon or on Shanks's Pony.

But things were getting better. Contemporary vestry accounts show a payment of £5. 12s. 8d. to an official called the superintendent of the road. By 1792 there were four turnpikes, north to Box, east to Melksham, west to Bath via Bathford and south-east to Trowbridge, with toll-gates at the approach to Bradford on Avon at Woolley Street, Bearfield (near the Castle Inn) and in St Margaret's Street at the north end of the Hall's almshouses. Charges ran from one penny for a single horse or other beast of burden, to 1s 4d for what must have been a rarity, a mechanically propelled vehicle. The turnpikes were removed in 1873, when roads became a local government responsibility under the Trowbridge Highway District.

In 1810 the canal which passed through Bradford on Avon was navigable from Bristol to the Thames. A brisk goods and passenger traffic soon developed, and for a few decades the town occupied a key position. Then came the railways, the canal's eclipse and our town's relapse into a relative backwater.

A directory of 1793 notes that no stage coach passed through the town and that goods were carried by Parsons's stage waggon from Bath, which called Mondays, Wednesdays, Thursdays and Saturdays. In 1837 there was a coach office in Pippet Street (now Market Street) run by Miss Fanny Wiltshire, (who also conducted an infants' school there); but in 1857 Bradford on Avon got its railway station, and stage coach days were over. But goods still went by road long-distance; a waggon left for London from the Queen's Head (now the Three Gables) in Bridge Street three times a week.

In 1828 the French had designed a horse-drawn public service passenger vehicle with seats lengthwise, facing each other, and an entrance at the rear. Because it was intended to be used by everyone, they called it an omnibus. The idea caught on, crossed the Channel and the vehicle came into general use here. From 1841 one ran daily between Bradford on Avon and Chippenham, calling at Holt, Melksham and Lacock. It was timed to connect with trains at Chippenham. Others ran locally to Bath, Trowbridge and Westbury.

There was a postal service in 1769; the postmaster was named John Renison. He was still in post in 1793; the *Universal British Directory* of that year records him not only as postmaster but also as clothier and grocer. In Renison's day the post came in from London and the intermediate towns daily at ten o'clock in the morning and went out at six o'clock in the evening. In 1837 there was a postman to deliver letters in the town in the morning and in Winsley and Westwood in the afternoon.

In the 1840s Joseph Rawling, the town's distinguished printer and non-conformist minister, seized the opportunity offered by Rowland Hill's reform of the previously expensive and inefficient service to get himself appointed postmaster and to move the post ofice next door to his printing and stationery business in Market Street.

In Rawling's day the first daily delivery in the town began at seven o'clock in the morning. There was a delivery of Salisbury and North mails at half past nine and a delivery of Bath and London mails at three o'clock in the afternoon. The office was open from nine in the morning to six in the evening and until eight o'clock in the evening on Saturday. On Sunday there was one delivery only and the office was closed at ten o'clock.

Right up to after the first World War there were deliveries on Sunday and the post office was open on Sunday morning.

A telegraph service was operated by the post office from 1870. In 1898 Bradford on Avon went on the telephone with the opening of an exchange by the National Telephone Company.

The Rope Walk.

SUGGESTED FURTHER READING

Besides the *Victoria County History* and Canon W H Jones's *Bradford on Avon* the following are suggested for readers with a general interest in Bradford's past:

Langdon, Gee: *The Year of the Map*, Compton Russell, 1976
Niblett, Bertram: *Memories of Bradford on Avon*, Wiltshire Library and Museum Service, 1981
Rawling, Charles: *The Bradford on Avon Pictorial Guide*, 1887
Bradford on Avon: a Pictorial Record, ed. Fassnidge and Maundrell, Wiltshire Library and Museum Service, 1983
John Leland's Itinerary: travels in Tudor England, ed. John Chandler, Alan Sutton, 1993
Bradford Settlement Examinations 1725-98, ed Phyllis Hembry for the Wiltshire Record Society, 1990
Terson, Peter: *Under the Fish and Over the Water*, Ex Libris Press, 1990

The following books are useful sources of information in their various fields:

Buildings
Nikolaus Pevsner: *The Buildings of England: Wiltshire*, Penguin, rev. ed., 1975

Churches
Wiltshire Meeting House Certificates 1689/1852 ed. John Chandler for the Wiltshire Record Society
The Journal of John Wesley ed. Nehemiah Curnock (8 volumes)
Mawby, Roger F: *Independent Meeting to United Church 1740-1990.*
Oliver, Robert W: *Baptists in Bradford on Avon*, 1989.
Rawling, Joseph: *The Biographical Records of Joseph Rawling*
Taylor, H M: *J T Irvine's work at Bradford on Avon* reprinted from The Archaeological Journal, Volume 129, for 1972 and published by the Royal Archaeological Institute.

Industry
Mann, J de L: *The Cloth Industry in the West of England from 1640 to 1880*, Alan Sutton, 1987
Ponting, Kenneth: *A History of the West of England Cloth Industry*
Rogers, Kenneth: *Wiltshire and Somerset Woollen Mills*, Pasold Research Fund Ltd, 1976
Rogers, Kenneth: *Warp and Weft: the Somerset and Wiltshire Woollen Industry*, Barracuda Books, 1987
Woodruff, William: *The Rise of the British Rubber Industry during the 19th Century*, Liverpool University
A Guide to the Industrial Archaeology of Wiltshire, ed. M C Corfield, Wiltshire Library and Museum Service, 1978

A TOWN TOUR

The following suggested walk is a fairly comprehensive circular tour which may be taken all at once (an hour to an hour and a half) or in two separate parts, of which Part I will take three quarters of an hour to an hour.

Part I Start at the station car-park. To the south-west, across the railway line, you can see Barton Farm and behind it the medieval tithe barn where our tour will finish. Budbury, where the Iron Age inhabitants and their Roman successors lived is to the north-west of here, roughly where the prominent rectangular building on the skyline (a former rug factory) now stands.

We go out of the car park to St. Margaret's Street where facing us is the Old Baptist Chapel and Hall's Almshouses. Near here stood the medieval leper hospital of St. Margaret which gave the locality its name. Walk down St. Margaret's Street towards Westbury House. The large building in the car park, built as a dye-house, is St. Margaret's Hall. The Quaker meeting house of 1718 and burial ground once occupied the parking area between the hall and the road.

Back in St. Margaret's Street, at Westbury House gardens, you are standing where the broad ford was and possibly where Cenwalh fought in AD 652. Cross the road. On the upstream side the town bridge dates back to at least the fourteenth century; the two pointed arches at this end of it are said to be late Norman. From the bridge on the down-river side view the excellent factory building of 1875 and note the small artificial 'island' in the foreground.

Cross the bridge, passing what was once the town lock-up or 'blind-house' to what was the old market place; the metal rings set in the parapet on the other side of the bridge were for tethering beasts awaiting sale. Passing the factory buildings on the right go a few yards up Silver Street and cross to where Coppice Hill and The Shambles join; this is where the original town hall stood till 1826. Number 6 Silver Street, the building faced with red brick is where John Wesley slept badly; the building is of stone so

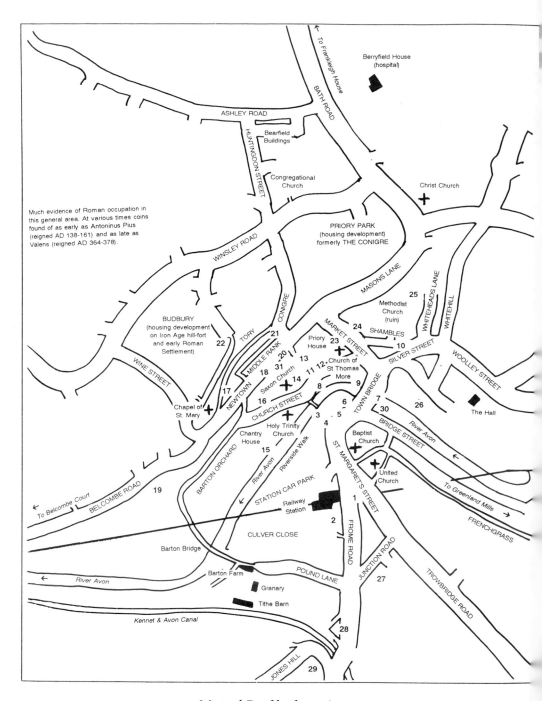

Much evidence of Roman occupation in this general area. At various times coins found of as early as Antoninus Pius (reigned AD 138-161) and as late as Valens (reigned AD 364-378).

Map of Bradford on Avon

the brick fronts added around the turn of the present century must have been meant as embellishment.

Further up the hill, on the same side, is a building (number 11) part of which dates back to about the fourteenth century. Stroll through the Shambles: the apparently timber-frame buildings are nothing of the kind, they are ancient stone buildings faced with wood and plaster in about the seventeenth century to make them look new.

Across the road on the corner of Market Street and Church Street is the Roman Catholic Church of St. Thomas More, built in 1855 as the town hall. Cross into Church Street and walk about fifty yards to Old Church House (Trinity Church Hall) on the right hand side. The building immediately before it, now a private house, was the Hobhouse, Phillott and Lowder Bank which, disastrously for the town, failed in 1841. Past Old Church House is Druce's Hill House and the building called the Dutch Barton. On the left is Abbey Mill and in front Abbey House. Ahead is the parish church and to the right the Saxon church. Orpin's House is a few yards ahead on the right and his reputed grave is immediately opposite just over the churchyard wall. In front is the Chantry House.

Key to numbers on map opposite:

1	Hall's Charity almshouses for men.	15	Kingston Place (former vicarage).
2	Probable site of St. Margaret's leper hospital (medieval).	16	Orpin's House.
		17	Lady Well.
3	St. Margaret's Hall (one-time dye-house).	18	Former Seven Stars Brewery and Malthouse.
4	Site of 1718 Quaker Meeting House and burial ground.	19	Wellclose House.
5	Westbury House.	20	Priory Barn.
6	Former Ford, probably the historic 'broad ford'.	21	Grove Meeting House.
		22	Budbury House (former rug factory).
7	Former blindhouse or lock-up (so-called chapel).	23	Pippet Buildings.
		24	Town Club, site of Maidenhead Inn and former Methodist chapel.
8	Abbey Mills		
9	Remains of former platform in the river for washing wool.	25	Quaker Meeting House.
		26	Site of Kingston Mill.
10	Site of earliest town hall.	27	Former Fitzmaurice Grammar School building.
11	Church House.		
12	Trinity Church Hall and Freemasons' Lodge.	28	St. Catherine's almshouses for women.
		29	Kennet & Avon Canal wharf.
13	Druce's Hill House.	30	Library and Tourist Information.
14	Abbey House, Abbey Yard and Dutch Barton.	31	The Ropewalk

Go up the narrow footpath past the weavers' cottages called Barton Orchard and up the steps to the street called Newtown. The fountain set in the wall is called Lady Well; this supplied water to cottages and houses in the vicinity before piped water came to the town in 1883. The adjacent fortress-like building, now converted to flats, was originally the Seven Stars malthouse and brewery. The stream which served Lady Well also served the brewery and powered a waterwheel there which is still in working order (but not accessible to the public).

If you do not wish to do the whole tour go back down the steps to Barton Orchard and follow the signpost to the tithe barn. From the tithe barn make your way back to the car park by following the path under the iron railway bridge.

Part II From Lady Well take the steep footpath (Well Path) up to Tory. Pause for breath and look out over the town to Westbury Hill and the Westbury White Horse. There, in AD 878, on a barren hillside (in Saxon parlance *ethandune*) King Alfred the Great won the decisive victory over the Danes under Guthrum which we call the Battle of Edington.

Go through the iron gates to visit the chapel of St. Mary. Then follow the footpath running round the side of the chapel which leads down to Wine Street, turn left and at the junction with Newtown turn right. This is Belcombe Road. Opposite the road called Belcombe Place is Wellclose House; the upper part of the John Wood frontage can be seen over the wall.

Continue along Belcombe Road about 400 yards for Belcombe Court on the right. Retrace steps for about 200 yards, cross the road, take the footpath down to and over the railway line and head for Barton Farm and the tithe barn. The Kennet and Avon Canal runs behind the barn, with the canal lock and wharf about a hundred yards away. From the tithe barn and Barton Farmhouse return to the station car-park by following the path under the iron railway bridge.

SOME BRADFORD ON AVON PLACE-NAMES AND THEIR ORIGINS

BARTON FARM, BARTON ORCHARD AND DUTCH BARTON

The word barton, which occurs frequently in English place-names, derives from Anglo-Saxon *beretun, bere* being barley and *tun* an enclosure. The term has been used variously down the ages, sometimes to mean not just a field of barley but also a farmyard and even a manor house. In Wessex it usually denoted a great farm; a small one was called a living.

BEARFIELD and BERRYFIELD

More likely to have been a barley field than one where there were bears or berries. *Bere* was Anglo-Saxon for barley, see above.

BUDBURY

English place-names with bury (Anglo-Saxon *burg or burh*) often denote a Roman or other pre-English fort and this is the case here. Canon Jones suggested that the name Budbury might derive from the presence of a chapel (St Mary, Tory), the element *bud* perhaps a corruption of Anglo-Saxon *bed* a prayer. Another suggestion has been that it was the site of a settlement of a Saxon chieftain called Budda.

BUDBURY TYNING

The word tyning derives from Anglo-Saxon *tynan* meaning to surround or hedge. It came to signify an enclosure.

BULL PIT

This street-name reminds us of the once very popular entertainment of bull-baiting or setting dogs to attack a bull tied to a stake. In 1835, in the face of strong resistance, bull-baiting was made illegal.

The passage leading from Church Street to Bull Pit was called Hang-dog Alley

CONIGRE HILL

The word conigre is Wessex dialect for a rabbit warren. Rabbits were encouraged to colonise. They were the poor man's equivalent of the rich man's ice-house, a valuable source of protein at any time and an aid to survival in the life-threatening winter months. (Readers familiar with Richard Adams's Watership Down will remember how, in their wanderings, the rabbits came upon one and but for the instinctive misgivings of Fiver and the mishap which befell Bigwig would have joined it). Sometimes conigres were maintained as game preserves, with shooting for sport from November to January. Such will have been the two Bradford conigres shown on the 1841 tithe map, Great Conigre which was part of the Priory estate, belonging at the time to Thomas Hosier Saunders, and Little Conigre which belonged to Thomas Wheeler. Great Conigre occupied what is now called Priory Park and the name of the lane leading steeply up from Newtown remains to remind us of it; Little Conigre was the part of Budbury lying behind the eastern end of Tory.

CULVER CLOSE
This is another reminder of medieval Bradford, recalling that hereabouts there was once a pigeon-house or dovecot belonging to Barton Farm. The word derives from Anglo-Saxon *culfre* meaning a dove or pigeon. The building will have been significant; in the Middle Ages only the Lord of the Manor and the parson were allowed to have one. This prerogative lapsed with the passage of time and by the sixteenth century it was established that any freeholder might have a dovecot on his land. Older Bradford houses will often be found to have recesses built into a wall to house a small flock of pigeons, which, like the wild rabbits enticed into the conigre (see above), made for a valuable and economical supplement to diet.

FRENCHGRASS
Frenchgrass is another name for sainfoin (*onobrychis sativa*). It thrives on light, dry, calcareous soil and hence does well here. It is particularly suitable for grazing sheep. Frenchgrass was at one time the name of a large pasture on the north-east side of Trowbridge Road; nothing now remains of it but the lane which bears its name.

HUNTINGDON STREET
Named after the chapel of the religious denomination called the Countess of Huntingdon's Connexion, an offshoot of Wesleyan Methodism.

KINGSTON ROAD
Formerly *frogmere*, conveying the strong suggestion of marshy ground in Saxon times (Anglo-Saxon *mere*, a pool of water) renamed in honour of the Duke of Kingston.

ST MARGARET'S STREET, ST MARGARET'S HILL etc.
Named after the former leper hospital of St Margaret.

View to Bradford on Avon from Victory Field.

NEWTOWN
The street called Newtown was 'new' in the late 1600s when it was a development (on land owned by the Methuen family) on the edge of the 'old' town. Workers from elsewhere will have been attracted to Bradford by the prospect of employment in the once more thriving clothing industry.

POUND LANE
Poundagium was the right or duty of impounding straying cattle, a term which included horses, sheep and other domestic animals. The pound was where they were held. Once impounded they were in the custody of the authorities and could only be retrieved on payment of a penalty and compensation for any damage done.

THE SHAMBLES
This little shopping street gets its name from the Anglo-Saxon word *scamel*, meaning a small bench or stool on which goods were exposed for sale. The goods displayed were usually meat and a shambles came to be in effect, a meat-market. It is probable that Bradfordians have shopped here for more than a thousand years.

SILVER STREET
There are streets so named in many Wiltshire towns besides Bradford. They are to be found in Calne, Malmesbury, Potterne, Salisbury, Trowbridge, Warminster and Wilton. As they are always in the town centre they were presumably so-called because they were where money changed hands a good deal. Bradford's Silver Street was not always so named. According to Canon Jones* it was formerly Fox Street and Gregory Street. The section leading from the town bridge marks the old Market Place.*

TORY and TORY PLACE
The name Tory derives from Anglo-Saxon *torr* meaning a high rocky place.

WOOLLEY STREET
Canon Jones tells us that a chapel dedicated to St Olave once stood at the corner of the lane leading to White Hill. St Olave Street became Tooley Street and by Jones's time Woolley Street.

The street has been, and sometimes still is, called Frying-pan Hill. The term Frying Pan is sometimes met with elsewhere as a field-name, denoting shape; thus, for example, in Wiltshire, Frying Pan Farm and Frying Pan Coppice, and in Berkshire (Basildon) Frying Pan Lodge (see The English Place-name Society's volumes XVI (Wiltshire) and (Berkshire)). It seems likely, therefore, that Bradford's Frying-pan Hill bordered on or led to a field of that name.

Many street-names derive from the presence of a family prominent locally in their day but now long forgotten. Such are Druce's Hill, Jones Hill, Kingston Road), Morgan Hill (before 1724 St. Margaret's Hill and now St. Margaret's Hill again), Whitehead's Lane, and White Hill. Some of these eponymous street-names have been lost: St. Margaret's Place was Bush's Alley, leading from Beasor Street, (which is now included in St. Margaret's Street).

Some streets have changed their names: Old Market has become part of Silver Street,

Some streets have changed their names: Old Market has become part of Silver Street, Mill Street has become Kingston Road and what is now called Market Street was formerly Horse Street and Pippet Street. What we now call Rosemary Lane was once Shocking Lane; Barton Orchard was Coal Ash Walk.

Some names have been lost; Hangdog Alley (which led from Church Street to Bull Pit), Pando Street, Slany Street (recorded in a document of 1367 relating to Barton Farm), Alto (or High) Street and Elbridge Lane (probably deriving its name, as, for example, the town of Elbridge in Kent does, from Anglo-Saxon *thelbrycg*, a plank bridge, which suggests the possibility that the Saxons had some sort of rudimentary bridge across the river, or, perhaps more likely, that they had one over a pool or wet ground (*cf. frogmere* above). The hill below the chapel of St Mary Tory was, until the eighteenth century, called Catshill ** or Catsholehill***. (The 'cats' living in the holes are more likely to have been martin-cats, with a price on their heads, than the domestic variety).

A Walk through Bradford on Avon: article in the Wiltshire Archaeological Magazine Vol.XX pages 306-322. But in 1748 Whitehead's Lane seems to have been called also Fox Street, see Wiltshire Archaeological Magazine Vol.XLI page 235.

** In 1745. Wiltshire Archaeological and Natural History Magazine vol 43, page 406

***Wiltshire Archaeological and Natural History Magazine vol 85, 1992 page 15

View across the Avon from Westbury Gardens.

INDEX

BRADFORD ON AVON MUSEUM SOCIETY

Bradford on Avon Museum opened in September 1990. Its aim is to preserve and display aspects of the natural and human heritage of the town of Bradford on Avon and of the surrounding countryside and villages which make up the ancient Hundred of Bradford.

The Museum's collections, still in their infancy, are slowly growing up to reflect the area's long history and industries. The displays centre upon the old Christopher Pharmacy, a shop that flourished in Silver Street for over 120 years and was lovingly rebuilt in the Museum, complete with its mahogany furnishings and rows of sparkling bottles and jars.

The Museum is run entirely by volunteers and depends upon grants, donations and subscriptions of members of the Bradford on Avon Museum Society, an independent charitable trust, with assistance from the Museums Service of Wiltshire County Council. New members are always welcome.

A royalty from sales of this book will be contributed to Bradford on Avon Museum Society – Publisher

Also available from Ex Libris Press:

UNDER THE FISH AND OVER THE WATER:
Bradford on Avon Community Play
by Peter Terson

Bradford on Avon Community Play portrays events which took place two hundred years ago – a period of rapid change in England and not least in Bradford, at the time an important centre of the West of England cloth industry, when mechanisation was seen as a threat to traditional methods of working.

The playscript is prefaced by an Introduction by the playwright who tells of his involvement, for the first time, in a Community Play, and of the genesis of this particular project. Included here, too, is a substantial piece compiled by members of the Community Play Research Group, which presents the facts, illustrated with archival material, of the play's background.

183 pages; ISBN 0 948578 26 2; Price £5.00

Written by Harold Fassnidge and published by Bradford on Avon Friends:

THE QUAKERS OF MELKSHAM: 1669-1950

Harold Fassnidge traces the history of Melksham Quaker Meeting from its origins. Vigorous and influential, the Meeting produced leaders at many levels. For the genealogist and family historian he has taken care to record what is known of those members whose names and doings, for one reason or another, feature in the Quaker records.

186 pages; ISBN 0 95194330 8; Price £4.50 Copies available from Ex Libris Bookshop, Bradford on Avon.